FURNITURE & FURNISHINGS

Melanie Paine

conran
OCTOPUS

First published in 1996 by

Conran Octopus Limited

37 Shelton Street

London

WC2H 9HN

This edition first published 1998

Commissioning Editor:	Denny Hemming
Senior Editor:	Catriona Woodburn
Art Editor:	Tony Seddon
Picture Researcher:	Rachel Davies
Production Controller:	Mano Mylvaganam, Jill Beed
Designers:	Isabel de Cordova, Amanda Lerwill
Artwork Visualizer:	Jean Morley
Illustrator:	Clare Melinsky

British Library Cataloguing-in-Publication Data.

A catalogue record for this book is available
from the British Library.

ISBN 1 84091 001 1

Printed in China

CONTENTS

Getting started 5

Decorative finishes for furniture 8

Preparation for decorative finishes 10

Applying decorative finishes 12

Using unusual materials 16

Soft furnishing 24

Using fabric 28

Seating 34

Cushions 36

Fastenings and edgings for furnishings 44

Covers for seating 52

Bedding 58

Bed-linen 60

Hangings and screens 64

Table settings 68

Table-linen 70

Sewing Guide 74

Stockists and suppliers 78

Index 79

Acknowledgments 80

Getting started

No decorating scheme will be successful unless careful
consideration is also given to the furnishings in the room.
However, this need not involve expensive purchases. Sofas
and chairs can be covered in a limitless range of beautiful
fabrics, while old wood and even metal furniture can take
on a new lease of life with the clever use of paint and
varnishing techniques. The choice of bed- and table-linen
offers still more opportunities to combine style and
comfort, and to contrast colours and textures.

Whatever the decoration on a room's walls, ceiling and floor, it is the style and coverings of the furniture within that will give the room its definitive character. At its simplest, a room with white walls and white floor, filled with furniture that has been upholstered in sumptuous velvets and bright, glassy coloured silks, will present a very strong, vivid style where colour is king. The eye will be drawn to the forms of the furniture, set off by the neutral, clean background.

The same room can be completely changed by the introduction of a different style of furniture decoration. To achieve warmth and texture in the same room, the emphasis shifts to creamy bleached wood furniture with cream-on-cream textured cushion fabrics and loosely draped white cottons over sofas and chairs, with perhaps a few warm red and terracotta touches – ties for the cushions or a painted chair.

When undertaking the decoration of a room, inevitably the walls and perhaps the floors will be tackled first. And when time, effort and money have gone into major refurbishment, attention to re-covering or redecorating the furniture may not be considered a priority for quite a while. This is a shame, for in addition to contributing in a major way to the final 'look' of a room, the pieces on or in which we sit, sleep, rest, eat, store and work figure as vital practical elements in our lives. It is important to account for these elements, not just in terms of budget and practicality, but also for the impact they make in the room.

Fabric is perhaps the most exciting and versatile way of covering and decorating the surfaces of furniture. Upholstering, wrapping, draping, cushioning – fabric comes alive when used imaginatively. From the finest, flimsiest linen to the most textured and mightiest of brocaded velvet, the potential of fabric for decorating and transforming furniture is unending. In addition to the fabric, there are braids, buttons and trimmings to truly jazz up a piece of fabric, define the curve of a sofa or accentuate the folds of curtains.

Fabric can also be decorated very successfully with paint or dye, in either a fairly controlled way, as with stencilling, or by using

▲ The bold use of colour creates a dramatic, Middle Eastern effect in this room. The varnished floor provides a neutral background for the rich, jewel-like fabrics draped on the sofa. The contrasting deep blue of the walls is also used around the door frame and in the tiles, helping to bring together different elements in the room.

▶ The strongest features in this room are light and space, which have been accentuated throughout. Furniture is grouped around the room to divide it into functional areas. The use of faded fabrics, the distressed paint effect on the cupboard and evidence of junk-shop finds add a nostalgic, tranquil feel to the room.

the more random method of hand-painted applications. Paint is also suitable for directly applying to the surfaces of furniture. Natural effects can be imitated or instant 'ageing' techniques applied for those who want a more battered, lived-in feel to their furniture. You can opt for the quick approach by using paint in a very loose way, such as colourwashing where layers are applied and reapplied to create the desired effect. The

finish can be changed easily to suit the mood of the rest of the room, altering the surface paint colour or 'texture' as easily as changing a cushion cover. Other paint techniques require more time and precision and because of this have a more permanent, perhaps less relaxed feel to them – the difference between a scrubbed pine table and an antique mahogany desk. Each has its place – it all depends on the effect you want to achieve.

Balance in all of this is crucial. Avoid over-doing a paint technique or using the same patterned fabric on every item in the room. Less is more. One beautifully colourwashed chair among a collection of pared-down fabrics can often be more effective than a riot of them. Although, in the right place, this too can be wonderful.

The position of furniture within a room is also very important. Don't feel that all large items of furniture should hug the walls – placing them on the diagonal and juxtaposing them can give unexpectedly pleasing results. In bigger rooms with numerous pieces of furniture, it helps to think in terms of group arrangements so that there are islands of furniture throughout the room, rather than many individual but slightly lost-looking pieces. Using the same colour, paint and fabric helps to link unrelated items throughout the room. Try different materials, be imaginative – but keep a balance.

▲ *Bleached cream, pale stone and stark white are relieved by a honey-toned floor in this harmoniously elegant room. Fabrics are the dominant feature of the room, together with the abundance of natural light that floods through the windows. The light reflects off the various surfaces to provide a sophisticated and relaxing environment.*

Decorative finishes for furnitur

Painting the walls of a room in a neutral colour or shade allows
the furniture free rein to make powerful colour statements.
Using different painting or varnishing techniques, furniture can
be transformed, creating dramatic visual effects within a room.
Wood, with its ability to transform itself with the application of
paint, varnish or wax, is extremely versatile and can be treated
in various different ways within the same room. Metal furniture,
too, can be enhanced with the application of different coverings
and the use of different paint-application techniques.

The choice of paint effects is vast: on the one hand, finishes such as fake rust or verdigris on wood or metal can add texture and 'weight', while a simple coat of varnish or beeswax may be applied purely to bring out the natural colour, grain and character of wood. For a subtle colouring effect somewhere in the middle, both varnish and wax come into their own when first mixed with a little powder colour or stain, and paint can produce a superb look when applied as a colourwash (see pages 14–15).

Built-in furniture – for example, alcove bookcases or cupboards – is often painted along with the rest of the wood in the room – invariably in an unadventurous, light off-white. Try painting such pieces in a different finish, such as a light colourwash or an antiqued finish, for a different effect.

Interesting surface decoration can transform a piece of furniture. A simple, plain chair could be painted in hot terracottas and a wild patterning of bright and bold stencilled borders, or in cool grey – worthy of an eighteenth-century Swedish interior – or in faded cream, russet and gold – befitting a nineteenth-century French salon.

Sometimes it is unwise to give single items of furniture, such as tables or chairs, a dramatic colour treatment if it makes them stand out in awkward isolation; you can, for example, achieve a stylish and harmonious look by simply painting a series of pieces in varying shades of cream.

Colourwashing is a wonderfully versatile way of putting paint onto a wood surface. On bare, untreated wood, diluted emulsion paint sinks in, lightly colouring the wood and allowing its natural qualities and grain to show through. The more diluted the paint, the more the character of the wood will come through. Two colours, one over the other, will give a richer finish. Light colours, especially on pale woods such as pine or light oak, can be used to give slight hints of colour, while a strong wash of inky black on a darker, grainier wood can be equally effective but a bit more dramatic. Rough and quite dark oak boards, for example, can take a fairly dark colourwash. The wash needs to be worked into the surface and, after a few

minutes, rubbed a little with a cloth. The deep browns of the wood will show through. A pale, chalky-white colour also creates a beautiful finish on more textured wood. The beauty of colourwashing is that the result is immediate and the technique easy.

With simple variations, attractive and widely different effects can be achieved using colourwashes. Paint narrow chequerboard borders along edges of, or panels in, the furniture. Alternate colours in wide bands across larger pieces. The beauty of this kind of painting is that it provides the opportunity for great adventure and experimentation with colour and texture. Create smart, chic pieces

in combinations of subtle chalky whites and bleached blues, or go wild with vibrant orange, mint green and deep indigo.

Metallic paints, if 'textured' a little, can give a wonderfully rich and exciting surface to furniture. Apply silver metallic paint to the prepared surface. Dilute black emulsion with water and a little detergent and, using a damp cloth, dab it over the surface, into mouldings or along edges, to build up a rich patina for dramatic effect. The silver-grey colour looks splendid against rich jewel colours – emerald, orange or deep burgundy. Try painting the legs of upholstered stools in this finish in combination with rich velvets and cord.

◄ *With a little imagination a tired piece of furniture can be magically transformed. This old chest of drawers, painted with bright seashore motifs and touches of gold, is lively and fun. It blends happily into a bright room where other accessories like candlesticks and lampstands are also painted for decorative effect.*

▲ *The beauty and warmth of polished wood show up well in this long honey-gold refectory table. The natural grain and patina of the wood are drawn out with waxing or varnishing, and contrast with the bleached-wood effect of the flooring. The rich colour and texture of the table are also emphasized by the neutral walls.*

Preparing surfaces for decorative finishes

▶ *The worn-out surface of this little cupboard may be the result of age, or it may have been finished to look old. In either case the effect is very appealing; but should such a piece require repainting or a new decorative effect, the old paint would need to be thoroughly removed and the surface rubbed down and washed.*

Make sure the surface you are to paint has been properly prepared beforehand, otherwise the effort of painting will be wasted. Unless you require a rough, unsanded surface with some of the imperfections that build up with the passage of time, a professional, smooth-looking finish is well worth the effort of good preparation.

Preparing and priming wood

For both wood and metal furniture it is important to remove all old paint and any varnish. Wearing rubber gloves, apply liquid or gel paint stripper with an old paintbrush, following the manufacturer's instructions. When the layers of paint begin to soften and bubble up, you can use a scraper to remove them from the surface – but take care not to scratch or gouge the surface of the wood. Stubborn areas can be rubbed with steel wool. Wash the surface down with either water or white spirit, depending on what type of stripper you have used.

It is possible to go to a professional wood-stripping company to have the item dipped in a caustic solution. It is not a bad idea to use this kind of service where appropriate: for example, to treat a large piece of furniture or an item with many layers of old paint,

as apart from the convenience, the fumes from the caustic solutions used in the stripping process can be overpowering.

Caustic solutions often leave the wood surface discoloured and slightly raised and rough, although a fine-grade sandpaper will restore the surface after several rubbings over. Either use sandpaper directly on the surface, applying pressure with your fingertips, or wrap it around a block. For simple curved mouldings, wrap it around a length of dowel. Before applying a finish, any knots in the surface should first be sealed, as they produce

resin and can cause discolouring of the finished paint surfaces. Apply one or two coats of knotting sealant over any knots, according to the manufacturer's instructions. If the surface needs some filling before applying a finish, lightly sand and apply a proprietary wood filler to match the grain of the wood. When dry, rub it down again until smooth.

Once the surface has been prepared it is not always necessary to prime it. Some finishes first require a layer of shellac and should not be primed. However, if you are going to paint it then it will need priming. This can be done using an oil-based wood primer, which traditionally comes in pink or white. Dilute the primer by using three parts primer to one part white spirit. Then, with a wide brush, apply it liberally over the surface. The next step is to apply undercoat using a clean brush. The surface is then ready for painting.

Preparing and priming metal

Preparing and priming metal are approached in much the same way as for wood, using specific solvents to remove the paint.

Spray paint can be removed with acetone; oil-based paints and varnishes with turpentine or white spirit; and French enamel varnish with methylated spirits. Use steel wool or a firm wire brush to remove the old paint layers and rust. Continue to rub the surface until it is completely smooth and clean. There are special zinc-based metal primers available for preparing the surface of metal for painting. A base coat of red oxide

Preparing wood

1 Apply liquid or gel stripper with an old brush and wait for the surface to bubble. Scrape off the softened paint.

2 Sand down the stripped surface. Use your fingertips to apply pressure for light sanding or for curved areas.

Preparing and priming metal

inhibits rust and protects metal, so it is ideal for treating garden furniture. Always remember to wear rubber gloves when using red oxide. Apply the primer in a single, even coat and leave it to dry for 24 hours.

Preparing and priming plastic

Wash the plastic surfaces down with a clean cloth and a solution of warm water and household detergent. Rinse the surface thoroughly with clean water, and dry it off completely before painting.

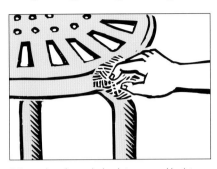

1 Use steel wool or a wire brush to remove old paint layers and rust from the surface.

2 Prime the metal before painting by applying a zinc-based metal primer to the surface. Allow 24 hours to dry.

Tools and equipment

For preparing and priming wood

- **Sandpaper:** in various grades from fine to rough, for removing old finishes and smoothing back wood filler.
- **Overalls, paper mask and rubber gloves:** for protection where the job is dusty and messy and may involve the use of solvents.
- **Flat scraper:** for removing paint.
- **Sponge with rough side, steel wool and small pointed knives:** for removing paint, including paint stuck into deep cracks.
- **Methylated spirits:** for removing French polish or shellac.
- **Paint stripper:** for removing other varnishes and paint.
- **Old paintbrush:** for applying paint stripper.
- **Patent knotting sealant (knot sealer):** to seal knots before priming.
- **Wood filler:** where wood requires filling and smoothing.
- **Undercoat.**
- **Primer.**
- **Sheets of plastic:** to protect the floor.

For preparing and priming metal

- **Methylated spirits:** for removing French enamel varnish.
- **Acetone:** for removing spray paint.
- **Turpentine or white spirit:** for removing oil-based paints and varnishes.
- **Steel wool:** for removing old paint layers and rust.
- **Metal primer.**

▲ *The magnificent red of the bath and curly metal washstand provides splashes of warmth in this cool grey-blue room. Metal furniture, especially if flaked with old paint and rust, requires some attention before painting. The rough surface of the bath was smoothed out after being rubbed, then primed, undercoated and covered with several layers of gloss paint.*

Applying varnish, glaze and stain

▲ *The natural colour of wood can be enhanced with an application of wax polish. If a bit more colour is required, you could try staining or glazing the wood. This rather battle-scarred bench has come up beautifully after being stained a rich chestnut colour. The intensity of the wall colour helps strengthen the wood's tones.*

Varnishes

Varnishes fall into different categories, depending on the solvent with which they can be diluted. These are: oil-based polyurethane (diluted with turpentine), water-based acrylic (diluted with water) and alcohol-based varnish (diluted with methylated spirits). Oil-based varnishes are available in matt, semi-matt or gloss finish, so choose carefully.

If you are using varnish simply to give a painted surface a good protective finishing coat, there are many household varnishes to choose from. However, polyurethane varnish has a tendency to go yellow. On many finished surfaces this will not matter, but on a pale colourwashed wooden table, for example, it is important not to ruin the effect of the subtle paint colour with the wrong varnish. Oil-based varnishes can be tinted with universal stainers or artist's oil paints.

Instead of oil-based varnish, you can use acrylic (water-based) varnish or those known as 'decorative' or 'copal' varnishes. These are more pleasant to work with, being quick-drying and having one quarter the toxicity of oil-based varnishes. PVA is also a useful varnish – white when liquid and clear once dry. It gives a good protective finish to most surfaces, particularly when using paper.

Shellac is a yellowish-brownish liquid which is not as tough as varnish but can be a useful sealant. French enamel varnish, made from bleached and chemically dyed shellac, looks much the same and can be dabbed on to bright brass to dull it down and give it an aged look. Originally brown, it comes ready-coloured in a wide range of shades and can be successfully diluted with methylated spirits. The liquid can stain and varnish wood in one application, but it dries very quickly so you have to work fast.

Applying varnish

Varnish should be applied with care to any finished surface. To facilitate drying, the air should not be damp so, ideally, you should varnish on a dry, warm day. Make sure the area you are working in is well ventilated and protect all surrounding surfaces with plastic sheeting before starting work.

Many types of brush may be used, including a standard paintbrush, and it is a good idea to experiment with various different types until you feel comfortable with one. Tin 'Glider' brushes are used for applying thin light varnishes; pointed brushes are best for using with shellac; while a chisel-headed lily-bristle brush will do for most other types of varnish application (other than shellac). Treat yourself to a good brush and look after it, cleaning it after every use. Never use varnish brushes for painting.

Coat the first third of the bristles with varnish. Take care not to wipe the brush against the rim of the pot as this causes bubbles. Transfer the loaded brush straight to the surface of the piece, brushing the varnish from the centre outwards. Remove any excess with a clean rag. Apply several coats of varnish, as necessary, brushing each one in a different direction. The final coat, especially if using a gloss varnish, will need a light rubbing down with fine wet or dry paper or fine steel wool.

Craquelure

To achieve a crackled surface effect, 'ageing' and 'crackle' varnish can be bought together as two separate bottles – one of which contains slow-drying oil-based varnish and the other quick-drying water-based varnish. These work against each other to create the decorative cracked finish.

First paint the surface of the furniture in a pale oil-based paint. When the base coat is completely dry, apply the oil-based varnish, according to the instructions, to the whole of the area you wish to 'crackle'. Use a soft fitch to ensure the layer is thin and smooth. Leave this to dry for about 45 minutes or until it is tacky to the touch. Apply the second varnish, also over the whole area. This can be left to dry naturally or aided with hot air from a hair dryer. As the top varnish dries, a network of cracks will form. After about an hour, when this process is complete and the varnish thoroughly dry, artist's oil paints or tinted oil glazes can be rubbed into

Craquelure

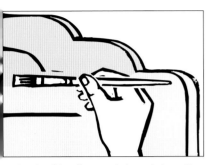

1 When the oil-based base coat is dry, apply the crackle varnish with a fitch. Once dried, apply the second coat.

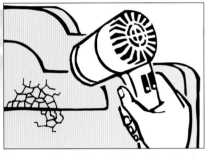

2 As soon as the varnish has dried the crackle will appear. Using a hair dryer will speed up the drying process.

3 When completely dry, rub tinted-oil glaze into the surface of the cracks with a soft cloth.

4 Rub off excess glaze with a clean cloth to leave dark cracks on a light background. Seal by applying a varnish.

the surface with a soft cloth so that the tint lodges in the cracks and accentuates them. When you are happy with the degree of colour and overall effect, rub off any excess glaze or oil paint not in the cracks and leave to dry for several days. Once dry, coat the area in shellac and/or an oil-based varnish.

Glazes

Oil glaze (also called scumble glaze) is an extremely versatile substance over paper or wood. It can be tinted with artist's oil paints and, when dry, will be translucent and smooth. Oil glaze behaves like a filmy translucent layer which, even if coloured slightly, will still allow colour beneath it to come through.

Creating an antiqued finish with oil glaze

Mix one part artist's oil paint to eight parts transparent oil glaze to create a murky tint. Antiquing glazes are best applied over a roughened surface so that the colour will sit in the wood grain and any surface scratches and cracks. If you have newly painted wood, you should sand or wire-brush it first to give

it a cracked appearance. Apply the glaze, brushing it out in different directions into a thin layer. Then use a rag to gently rub it off in patches, leaving the glaze in the cracks of the surface to create a mottled effect.

As well as applying tinted-oil glaze to plain or painted wood, it can be applied over photocopied images and newspapers that have been glued onto furniture such as screens. This will make paper look as if it is old parchment. Finish off with a coat of clear varnish to give lasting protection.

Stains

Wood stains will colour wood but, unlike varnish, they will not seal it. Wood stains can be used as plain colour or, more decoratively, painted on surfaces in geometric patterns to imitate marquetry. Look at tile patterns in historic houses or church interiors for inspiration. To stain wood, first mark out the pattern by lightly scoring the wood with a knife. This helps to prevent the different coloured stains from seeping into their neighbouring sections. Apply the stain with a brush and allow to dry. Finish with several coats of varnish to seal the wood.

◄ *A painted surface that looks cracked and aged by both time and use can be achieved using the craquelure technique. The gently broken surface it produces, especially when used with paints in pale colours, can be given a further ageing effect with the addition of a coloured antiquing glaze rubbed gently into the surface.*

Applying paint and wax

Paint on wood

Colourwashing

Exactly as its name implies, colourwashing involves the application of a 'wash' of water-based paint onto a wood surface to create thin, transparent layers of colour.

Build up colour and texture bit by bit, painting over previous layers and moving the paint around with the brush. The application of the paint can be quite rough and uneven to give a lively, 'loose' effect. If, however, you want the finish to be quite even, apply a final coat in a paler colour. Take care to 'contain' the unevenness by setting the finished piece

▶ The wonderful patina and character of weathered slabs of old wood have been enhanced by using a liming technique. The creamy white wash sits in the grainy surface of the wood, but still allows the original colour of the wood to show through. The white colour scheme of the room is complemented by the use of this technique.

of painted furniture against a clean-looking background. Colourwashing with three colours achieves a rich, intense depth.

Colourwash with a wax resist

Painted or colourwashed furniture can be given a slightly beaten-up, weathered look using a wax resist. Wax resists the paint and can be rubbed off at the end of the process to reveal the base layer – whether it is the original wood, or a painted or enamel-varnished surface.

Beeswax polish, or rubber glue that can be removed easily, should be applied over the base coat with a small brush in streaks or

blobs. The more worn out the finish you require, the more wax or glue you should apply. Once dried, paint on a layer of emulsion paint and allow this to dry overnight. Then apply subsequent diluted layers. When the last coat has dried, use an old cloth and a scraper to remove the wax or glue, exposing the base and other layers of paint. Finally give the whole piece a light sand.

Wax on wood

Liming

Liming is an effective technique used to enhance the beauty of the wood, leaving a white residue in the grain and cracks and a subtle white sheen over its surface. Choose a wood that has a noticeable and attractive grain. Oak and ash are two good examples of woods that have an 'open' grain and take the white liming paste or wax particularly well. However, if you are prepared to thoroughly wire-brush the surface of a piece of pine furniture (pine has a 'closed' grain), the white waxy residue will be equally effective. All wood surfaces should be lightly wire-brushed first to open the grain. Work the brush in the direction of the grain.

Ready-made liming wax is the easiest to use, and it should be applied using a fairly stiff brush. The idea is to coat the wood and allow the wax to settle in its cracks, splits and grain. Once the wax has dried, smooth over the surface with a cloth, taking care not to lift the wax out.

Colourwash with wax resist

1 Apply the beeswax polish or rubber glue to the surface of the furniture. Brush it on in streaks with a small brush.

2 When dry, paint a layer of emulsion over the surface. Allow to dry again and then apply further diluted layers.

3 After the final layer has dried, use an old cloth and scraper to expose the base and other layers of paint.

Verdigris

▲ *This truly majestic piece of furniture has intricate metalwork encrusted with old peeling paint and rust, which wonderfully complements the rich textures of the kilim and the velvet of the cushions and upholstery. Aged paintwork can be re-created effectively by paint techniques which imitate rusted, bleached or otherwise battered surfaces.*

1 A few small patches of yellow ochre are dabbed across the table's finished paintwork using a thin artist's brush.

2 Gently pour water over the surface of the table to expose some of the under layers of paint.

3 Sprinkle whiting powder over the damp surface of the table and press onto the surface and into the mouldings.

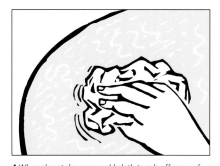

4 When almost dry, use an old cloth to rub off some of the whiting powder. When dry, seal with diluted PVA.

Paint on metal

Verdigris

Pale-green-topped buildings are a common site in most towns and cities. The sea-green colour is the naturally occurring corrosion of copper, brass or bronze. Verdigris, as the effect is called, takes time to develop and although items can be left outside for the weather to do its work, it is possible to cheat and achieve authentic-looking verdigris by using paint and paste.

The technique is suitable for metal or plastic items such as picture frames, candlesticks and lamp bases, and for furniture, but it has to be worked onto a horizontal surface as the paste will not stick to a vertical one. If you are working on a metal-framed table, for example, you will need to do each part of the frame separately, turning the table so that the painted surface is always horizontal.

The base for the work should be a bronze-brown colour, so first paint the item with a suitable shade of paint, French enamel varnish or shellac and allow this to dry. Apply a wash of deep-green emulsion (diluted one part emulsion to four parts water) and leave this to dry. If necessary, apply a second coat.

You now need to make up two verdigris pastes, one using mint-green emulsion and the other a pale blue. Mix methylated spirits into each of the paints (one part spirit to two parts emulsion). Using a sieve, mix in plaster powder or whiting until you have smooth and fairly stiff pastes.

The two pastes should be applied to the painted surface randomly, building up varying degrees of texture. Don't be too precise about applying the paste and leave some areas of the basecoat showing through. While this is drying, use a thin artist's brush to apply a little well-diluted yellow ochre acrylic paint in small random patches across the surface. When dry, gently pour water over the whole surface, to expose some of the layers beneath.

Sprinkle some whiting or powder over the damp surface, pressing it into the surface and into any mouldings. When almost dry, use a cloth to rub off some of the powder so that the layers underneath show. The finished result should look like the patinated metal it is imitating. When dry, seal with diluted PVA. For a really hard-wearing surface, apply a matt polyurethane varnish. Creating a look of rusted metal can be achieved in a similar way, using brown and red paints.

Using unusual materials

▲ *Bold and whimsical, these plastic blown-up cushions with their emphatic rows of brightly coloured circles are a throwback to the 1960s but they work surprisingly well in this otherwise deliberately restrained interior. Balance these unusual materials with something more familiar to create maximum impact.*

This section salutes a small but exciting selection of surprising and unlikely materials that can stunningly alter the surface of a piece of furniture. Neither fabric nor paint, there is no collective term that can be used to describe such diverse materials as paper, plastic, jute fibre, wire mesh, glass and ceramic, but used individually or even together they break the boundaries of what is both familiar and predictable in interior furnishing.

Contrast and texture, and the interplay between them, are the keys to using these materials with style and verve. Keep in mind balance and symmetry – a small amount of something unexpected usually goes a long way! Consider hard and soft surfaces together and juxtapose matt opacity with cool glassy light-reflecting surfaces. Imagine, for example, shiny plastic or metal gauze against a smooth rubber or linoleum floor. With

such diversity, it is to be hoped that the days when almost every surface was covered in a floral chintz fabric are dim and distant.

While working with such unusual materials will not be to everyone's taste, it is undoubtedly true that using metal, plastic and paper, for example, as materials for furnishings, will be a challenge to your imagination and perspective. Imagine a glass-topped table draped in a shimmering, gauze-like, finely meshed metal. It would make a wonderful and unusual backdrop for a collection of glass objects. Put a swathe of shot silk beneath the metal and you have a stunning combination. Ribbons or tassels can be tied to sheets of wire mesh for added texture. Metal-framed chairs wound with jute fibre or twisted straw fronds provide fabulous textural contrast.

Mixing and experimenting are the keys to success when using any material with which you are unfamiliar. Some of these, and their applications, are by no means new: mosaic, for example. And although paper is a familiar material, using it as a covering for furniture opens up a new dimension.

We are continually drawing on past styles and themes in attempts to find new ways of decorating surfaces. While few of us have the inclination or ability to re-create the splendid mosaic masterpieces of the ancient Roman artisans, we may well consider and be influenced by their use of pattern and colour in our own more modest creations.

Classic, timeless pieces can be given a twist in new materials. For example, the familiar shape of an upholstered club armchair, with its solid proportions, is retained yet transformed if sculpted from twisted metal or corrugated cardboard.

Wit and a hint of mischief may occasionally take over from practicality – and why not, when wearied by mass-production and safe, 'co-ordinating' schemes? Plastic inflatable cushions for most of us may look best floating on the shimmering surface of a swimming pool, but we are already being introduced to worktops made from plastic waste. So, in pride of place – perhaps on the *chaise longue* so exquisitely crafted from recycled plastic containers – why not a plastic inflatable bolster cushion?

◀ *The surprising use of stunningly coloured, solid glass to make this 'tablecloth' and matching stool provide a dramatic focal point in the room. The equally unusual orange-yellow light fitting over the table, and the large, uncurtained window contribute to the glass theme.*

Paper

Although it is more usually found on the walls of a room, paper is a very exciting medium to use on furniture – whether wood, metal or plastic. In its many forms, it transfers particularly easily to flat, smooth surfaces such as table tops, drawer fronts, cupboard panels and even wooden chairs. Other than glue to paste it to the surface, the only other requirement is a top coat or two of clear varnish, to preserve it from tearing.

Paper can be matt and rough like newsprint, smooth and shiny as on a magazine cover, printed, embossed, plain, silver, thin, transparent, and much more besides. Once you begin to identify the different types available – even those in everyday use – its versatility becomes instantly evident. It offers numerous decorative possibilities, for while it can, of course, be cut with a knife or pair of scissors, torn, folded or scrunched, it can also be stitched and even woven.

Do not assume that paper cannot be a sturdy material. The famous Lloyd Loom chairs are made from twisted paper woven together, resulting in a form that is very strong and hard-wearing. In addition, some types of card – corrugated, for example – are sufficiently rigid to make free-standing pieces, or 'cut-out' cases that may be dropped over or applied to a timber frame – as seating, for example. To achieve a light-hearted decorative element you could also explore the technique of *trompe l'oeil* by painting yourself a magnificent carved wood table or a whimsical chair on a free-standing silhouette of card.

Lay cut or torn pieces of paper on a flat surface under sheets of glass, or perhaps overlay fine black-and-white newsprint with tiny pieces of coloured metallic foil from sweet wrappers in a mosaic pattern. Try weaving strips of multicoloured images from magazine pages between strips of plain coloured paper to create a flat chequered surface which can be laid or pasted, like a mat, on tables or cupboards. Folded strips of newspaper could be woven in the same way – and complemented by brown paper. Such a monotone surface lends itself to cool, clear interiors where natural materials, such as wood, stone or terracotta, feature.

▲ *Painted and decorated paper has been used to cover the top, sides and drawer fronts of this unusual chest of drawers. This simple effect works particularly well on flat surfaces, where it is easy to manipulate the paper and achieve neat folds and edges. Another advantage is that if you don't like it, you can rip it off and try something else.*

Textured paper

For a smart and sophisticated surface use simple embossed letters or motifs on a beautifully hand-crafted sheet of paper. You can order an embossing press with your own initials or customized image, and the advantage of heavy handmade paper is that it has some texture and thickness. Another simple method of adding texture to paper is to use a sewing machine to punch lines across its surface, but take the thread out of the machine first! The results resemble punched metalwork and can be cut to fit areas such as cupboard door panels.

There are numerous types of specialist handmade paper on the market, many of which have beautiful and unusual textures, while others resemble stone or granite. They are made from recycled paper, often with a scattering of plant pieces, flower petals or onion skins. Some are really lovely, and make wonderful decorative material. Although they appear fragile, they are actually quite strong. For protection on a table surface, however, the sheets will need laying under glass.

Pleating paper

Pleated or folded paper can be used behind glazed cupboard doors as a less-expensive alternative to fabric. Use a crisp, smooth paper or thin card and mark with tiny dots along the top and back edge of the paper. The dots need not be equally spaced but must line up on both edges. Fold on alternate sides, following the marked fold lines. Use a bone letter opener to crease the fold lines. Attach the folded sheets to the timber frame of a glazed door using tacks.   ▷

◄ *Paper is an extremely versatile material available in a huge range of different colours, textures and weights. Here, reproduction-antique printed paper has been used to cover the lampshade and the wallpaper. Be bold and create unusual effects by experimenting with various types of paper on different surfaces.*

Paper can be applied directly to a smooth, clean surface using PVA glue, diluted 1:1 with water. A large sheet of newsprint or printed wallpaper could be used across a table top, for example, or if you don't wish to paste directly onto the table, cut a piece of plywood or MDF to the same size and wrap it in the paper. Seal the finished surface with the PVA solution. Alternatively, assemble smaller pieces of plywood, cut to the size of a standard ceramic tile, each covered in a different coloured or printed paper, and lay the paper-covered 'tiles' together on a recessed table top. Protect the surface with a sheet of glass.

Maps are fun to use on or over furniture. Look for old examples in second-hand book-shops, or huge, brand-new, brightly coloured world maps. These are great for children's rooms or more informal, relaxed spaces. Again, use diluted PVA, both to stick down the paper and to seal its surface.

Plain papers can be dyed, painted, stained, marbled or printed on before being used. Children's paintings, pasted onto the sides and base of a simple wooden box and then sealed, would make a fun addition to a play-room. Use acrylic paints on the paper as they will not mix with the glue.

The inside of plain pine chests can be given a lift by using a lining paper inside the lid and in the box itself. Wallpapers with old or contemporary designs are excellent, as the paper is quite tough and the selection of pat-terns available is wide.

A clever way of brightening up and com-pletely transforming a fairly dull chest of drawers or small seed chest would be to cover all the drawer fronts with paper. Take a pic-torial scene – *toile de Jouy* wallpaper would be a good start – and cut the pattern into a grid, one for each drawer. You will need to allow sufficient paper to turn around the sides of each drawer front. Stripes or tartan papers would be equally effective. For a children's room, for example, alternate different bold colours. Remove drawer knobs first. Apply the paper using PVA and make sure the surface is smooth and wrinkle-free. After leaving the paper enough time to dry (and taking care not to tear it), carefully screw the knobs back on again.

Decoupage

This technique is the decoration of surfaces with paper cut-outs. Interesting effects can be achieved by photocopying single images, enlarging or reducing them according to the size of the item you plan to cover, and cutting them out. Almost any printed paper that you can cut and paste can be used: look for old engravings of flowers or fruit, or architectural details for a classical theme, pieces of newspaper, playing cards, old doc-uments, glossy magazine covers, wallpaper borders or elements of more intricate pat-terns such as old fabric or wallpaper designs. For traditionalists, multicoloured floral designs and fat little cherubs will follow the Victorian style – they used decoupage on just about everything. Also interesting – for a

▲ *This is a delightful and original way to make a feature of a dull hallway or a dreary corner. Every surface is covered with an unusual paper. The toning base colours of the floor, skirting board and wallpaper form a unifying background, allowing the printed paper on the table and the pattern on the wallpaper to really stand out.*

kitchen surface perhaps – are hardware cata-logues depicting pots, pans and other culinary gadgets. Cupboard handles and mouldings can be photocopied, painted or stained if required, and then pasted into place onto the flat surface of a plain cupboard front. When assembled, the effect is that of a fake dresser or cabinet.

Letters or numbers also make interesting decoration. Use varying styles and sizes cut out from magazines, newspapers or posters, and dot them all over a surface such as a large desk. A background of plain brown parcel paper can be used for contrast. Sheets of dif-ferent typeface styles also look good when pasted together.

How to decoupage

Use a scalpel to cut out the paper or photo-copied images, and a 1:1 dilution of PVA glue and water for pasting and varnishing. Also useful is a decorator's brush for pasting and a smaller artist's brush and diluted emulsion paints (or acrylics) for colouring black-and-white photocopies.

Cut out the images on a hard, flat surface, ideally a cutting board, using the scalpel. Prepare the background: for example, news-paper, brown paper or a painted surface. Coat the paper cut-outs on both sides with the diluted PVA. Position the pasted paper and brush over. When it dries the paper will shrink a little. Paint the image with diluted paint or 'antique' it (see pages 12–13) if this is in keeping with the effect you want.

▲ *Scraps of old letters and music scores have been layered and pasted directly onto the newly painted cream surface of this chest of drawers to give an unusual but very imaginative look. The overall effect, reinforced by the neutral colour of the chest and the fireplace is restful and harmonious.*

Decoupage

1 Select various images from newspapers or magazines and, using a scalpel, carefully cut them out.

2 With a paintbrush, coat both sides of the cut-out shapes with a 1:1 mix of water and PVA.

3 Position the pasted cut-outs on the surface you are covering and then brush the shapes over with the mix.

Mosaic

As a decorative art form, mosaic has been around for thousands of years. Little bits of stone, pebble, glass and even shell have been used to embellish walls, floors and other surfaces, both inside and outside, in all sorts of buildings that range from the grandest of cathedrals to the humblest of dwellings. Throughout history, from the time of the ancient Greeks and Romans, mosaics have

depicted figurative scenes as detailed as paintings or tapestries. Huge areas were covered in fragments of ceramic, precious or semi-precious stones which had borders of intricate abstract patterns running around the central image. As a purely abstract art form, mosaic ran riot during the Art Nouveau period in Europe, with roofs, courtyards, columns and almost every available surface

covered in startlingly bold and detailed designs by skilled practitioners who embraced its versatility and vibrancy.

In contemporary interiors mosaic is being re-employed as a means of decorating surfaces. On furniture it can be used to embellish table tops, mirror frames, bed-headboards or even chairs. The pieces that traditionally formed mosaic are known as

▶ *Mosaic is a time-old tradition in most cultures. Here, a pattern has been pieced together and set into the top of the round table. The mosaic effect is echoed in the background in the tiles placed around the kitchen area.*

Mosaic

1 Break up the pieces for your mosaic into small chips. You may need to cut them again to fit into the edges.

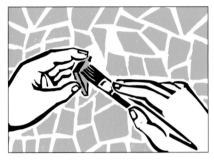

2 Once the pattern has been devised, apply glue to the back of the mosaic pieces and position them.

3 Apply grout across the surface of the mosaic. Spread evenly, filling in the gaps between each piece of mosaic.

4 Before it dries, wipe off any excess grout smeared across the surface of the mosaic with a clean cloth.

tesserae or 'smalti' – small coloured glass or enamel blocks. Tesserae can be bought from specialist suppliers, but it is possible to use a whole variety of materials in mosaic work: interesting effects can be achieved using broken pieces of household ceramic tiles or crockery, glass, perspex or even mirror.

Most surfaces, if prepared correctly, can take mosaic. You may need to score some surfaces, such as metal, in order for glue or cement to take; and wood, plywood or MDF must be sealed first with a 1:1 solution of water to PVA. Hardboard for a table top, for example, can be bought to your specifications from some hardware stores. However, you can apply mosaic directly to the surface of furniture. Keeping the work horizontal until the grout has dried is important. If you have ever tiled a floor or wall, the approach is much the same, but simpler.

Arranging the tiles

Designs, abstract or figurative, may be first mapped out on the base or you can piece the pattern together as you go along, creating a kaleidoscope of colour. For a random design, begin by playing with the segments on the surface of the table or board, moving them around until a pleasing pattern forms. For thicker tiles you may need to score and snap some of the segments that are to edge the board; for thinner tiles and tesserae, use tile nippers to create curves for your pattern.

Crockery or larger tiles can be broken and subsequently cut into more refined shapes. Alternatively, you can use the randomly broken segments in a loose abstract arrangement, but be prepared to use more grout between each bit. Should you wish to embark on more adventurous mosaic projects with harder materials such as marble or smalti, it is worth investing in a hammer and hardie – essentially a small anvil against which the piece is held while a sharp-edged hammer is brought down onto its surface, thus breaking the piece.

Gluing and grouting

Once the pattern has been decided and the pieces cut, apply glue to the back of each piece and stick them down onto your hard-

▲ *Here is a wonderful use of mosaic – insetting random and regular patterns within the panelled sections of this wooden bed frame. The decoration is pleasingly restrained and quite beautiful in its simplicity. Small ceramic tiles in tidy rows perfectly balance the irregular pieces of broken tile in the centre.*

board or other surface. Leave to dry. Then mix up the grout, following the instructions, or use ready-mixed grout. Grout can be coloured if desired, using water-based or acrylic paints, which should be added in small amounts to the dry powder type.

Apply the grout across the surface of the mosaic and spread evenly, filling all the gaps between the sections of tile or glass. Before it dries, wipe off the excess with a damp cloth. The piece should be left to dry for at least 24 hours and then the surface cleaned and polished with a clean cloth.

Soft furnishing

Everyone for whom fabrics are a real passion
will find the excitement of handling textiles and
the exploration of their potential – both practical
and decorative – absolutely all-embracing. From
earthy-coloured wool tartans to shimmery, lustrous
silks, the inspiration and fascination are the same.
This has, perhaps, something to do with the tactile
qualities of cloth, with its origins and history, and
with its many and varied forms.

Weave

Both the structure of a weave and the choice of yarn affect the final character of the cloth. Different weave structures used on the same yarn will produce significantly different finished fabrics. Smooth cotton sateen, for example, looks nothing like muslin, although both are made of cotton. This is almost entirely because of the way each is woven.

Plain weave is the simplest and most obvious method of weaving a length of cloth. The weft threads (those travelling widthways across the loom) go under and over alternate warp threads (those travelling lengthways across the loom). On the next row, the warp thread travels over the weft thread where previously it went under, and under it where it went over. Alternating row by row, this pattern repeats itself.

In most woven cloths, the warp threads are assembled on a loom first (in a variety of forms) and then the weft threads are woven through them. In some cloths, however – jacquard cloth, for example – the weave is very much more complex. Indeed, jacquard cloth is produced on its own special loom, from which the cloth takes its name.

Yarn

Different yarns – of cotton, linen, wool or silk – are responsible for giving particular characteristics to fabrics. Yarns may be mixed in one cloth for various reasons: to add more strength or lustre, or for economic reasons.

Cloth may be dyed once woven (piece-dyed) or the yarn may be coloured before the weaving process begins. In addition, an infinite variety of pattern can be achieved by printing on cloth. Complex modern printing methods can achieve stunning effects: computer-generated imagery is used to print holograms onto cloth, for instance, and computers are also used in weaving.

Fabric as a soft furnishing

Applying fabrics to furniture and using them for furnishings are endlessly rewarding; they are so versatile, and full of scope. There are many reasons for wanting to cover a sofa in fabric, for instance: perhaps for mundane practical reasons, or for a change of mood ▷

◀ Long streams of billowy fabric in gorgeous, jewel-like colours flow down from the ceiling and demonstrate how stunning effects can be achieved with the bold use of soft furnishings. The light just visible through the material creates the illusion of an added dimension to the room.

▲ Different fabric textures mingle happily when these blue and white cushions are thrown together in an attractive heap in the corner of a day-bed. The blues are matched in the stripes of the seat cover, while the intricately woven white cushion covers create a link with the white-painted bedstead.

or lifestyle; for comfort – replacing some much-loved but worn-out covers that let the itchy stuffing through – or perhaps to follow the ever-changing whims of fashion. Imagine a plain and simple sofa and cover it, in your mind's eye, in pristine white cotton first of all. Then imagine it transformed with a covering of multicoloured kilim. It can become something different again if floral prints are introduced – or tartans or paisleys.

Customizing fabric

New 'fabrics' can be created by mixing and joining old pieces together, rather as you would with patchwork. Borders and edges can be created for fabrics using strips of other cloths, or braids or ribbons – themselves small textiles. Apply paint to create pattern and texture, and mix wallpaper paste into the paint for wonderful textural effects (see pages 30–33) which tend to transform not only the surface but the entire cloth.

Different weights of fabric can be combined: heavy wool can be stitched in strips between narrow lengths of flimsy cotton, for example, and an entirely new fabric will be constructed. The alternating weight creates an interesting movement when it is handled, and this in turn may suggest new, unexpected uses that neither fabric could offer alone.

Fabrics can be embellished with beads, fringes and tassels in varied and glorious ways. Swirling patterns of shiny silk can crisscross a surface of matt cotton and utterly transform it. Braids and cords can be added to fabric edges to give definition, texture and a touch of luxury. The woven detail of some miniature textiles (passementerie) is quite breathtaking, but use them to uplift a plain fabric, for one of the joys of using them is that, until you are close to them, you cannot see the intricate threads and knots and thus they have an inbuilt element of surprise.

Although some types of fabric will lend themselves to particular settings or uses, exciting and unexpected effects can be achieved by shifting them around and trying less predictable applications. A 2.5cm (1in) border of tiny checks of black-and-cream ribbon running around the edge of a throw of creamy cashmere, for example, draws the

▲ *The wide range of fabrics used in patchwork and appliqué throws and cushion covers offer a good opportunity to introduce colours and colour combinations into a room. The muted tones in the room above required a splash of vibrancy to add interest and this was amply provided by the various cushion materials.*

eye and enhances the tactile quality of the original fabric. It provides both a quiet definition and a striking note. In other instances, it is a matter of improvisation and surprise. Try, for example, combining a creamy linen with a rough hessian band, or a canary-yellow velvet with a traditional wool tartan. While these two pairings would not sit comfortably with each other, if you change the colour of the velvet to a rich chocolate brown, and the tartan to one featuring earthy reds and ochres, a much more cohesive look appears. It is colour that provides the link and gives you the opportunity to be bold and mix different patterns and styles together. Alternatively, keep to the similar fabric types and use clashing colours. Colour can be fashionable; certain colour groups come in and out of fashion. One minute it may be chic to be all-over neutral but the next everything must be brilliantly bright. New fabric designs are constantly flooding the marketplace,

while retuned old designs continue to surprise and delight. The combination of change and familiarity is what makes using fabrics so exciting, for each new introduction creates an entirely new feel.

When selecting fabrics, do not confine yourself necessarily to traditional furnishing fabric suppliers. Be more inspired and try specialist shops or market stalls; look at stores that sell artist's canvas or Indian saris. It is relatively easy to find antique fabrics too. They do come up at auction, and although they can often be prohibitively expensive or perhaps too fragile or damaged to use for anything major, they can be combined with other cloths or used in a way that does not jeopardize their continued life. It is worth looking at ethnic fabrics too: African barkwork or Native American beadwork, for example, may be used in an exciting way in combination with contemporary machine-made fabrics or against unexpected surfaces.

◀ *No attempt has been made to match or co-ordinate any of these clashing fabrics and yet the combinations make for an exciting array of colours and print sizes. Damask mixes with a leopard print which mingles with a floral backdrop – but the uniting factor is the drama provided by each of the bold fabrics.*

Directory of furnishing fabrics

Textiles are all woven, even if they have pattern applied later. Non-woven anomalies are included here, as we tend to think of them as fabrics. More unusual textiles, such as felt or suede, often provide a greater number of decorative possibilities.

Appliquéd fabrics are pleasing to use as furnishings. Combined with patchwork, for example, a very personalized cloth can be created. **4**

Crewelwork fabrics, which use stitching to create a surface pattern, often on a ground cloth of thick woven cotton, are wonderfully textural.

Fake fur can be startlingly effective as upholstery fabric too.

Woven and non-woven fabrics

Bouclé
Suitable for upholstery, characterized by a looped surface.

Brocade
Originally woven from silk, with rich surface pattern and matt background. Gold threads were laid in to highlight.

Broderie anglaise
Cotton fabric, usually white, with embroidered cut-out 'lacy' pattern.

Calico
Cream, plain-woven cotton, originally from India. Can be bleached white.

Cambric
A firm, fine, creamy, plain-woven cotton, often treated to give it a slight sheen. Used for inner covers for pillows and duvets, as its close weave prevents feathers from escaping.

Canvas
Also called duck, a strong, heavy fabric in linen or cotton, it is woven to make it waterproof. Can be dyed or bleached; used for ships' sails and awnings.

Chenille
From the French, meaning caterpillar. Originally made from wool or cotton, it has a thick, soft pile that drapes well.

Corduroy
Traditionally heavy, cotton fabric with evenly spaced, ribbed pile running down the length of the cloth.

Damask
Traditionally woven for sophisticated table-linens. Damask is a fine fabric, with a reversible pattern created by the weaving process. Usually it is one colour throughout.

Dobby cloth
Woven on dobby loom, with simple, small, regularly repeated woven motifs.

Doublecloth
Strong, reversible fabric, comprising two separate but interwoven cloths.

Felt
Made from a mass of wool or hair pulped together until matted and shrunk. Does not fray when cut.

Flannel
A smooth fabric made from wool, traditionally used as suiting but good for upholstery too.

Gauze
Soft, sheer fabric; some warp threads are twisted for a very slight texture.

Gingham
Plain-weave cotton: checked pattern combines white and one other colour.

Hessian
Coarse-fibred jute cloth used for sacking – also upholstery. Firmer, narrow widths are used as webbing tape.

Jacquard
Intricately patterned, reversible fabric; takes name from French loom. **2**

Jute
Fibrous material from plant stems, used as yarn for weaving hessian.

Kilim
Woven like tapestry, made from cotton or wool, and characterized by narrow slits between the areas of pattern. **3**

Lace
Delicate openwork intricately patterned fabric, made by twisting and knotting threads. Traditionally cotton.

Linen
Strong cloth woven from flax. Tends to crease, but this can look attractive.

Madras
Inexpensive, brightly checked and striped, plain-weave Indian cotton.

Moiré
A finely ribbed fabric, usually silk or acetate, with rippling surface pattern.

Muslin
Plain-weave cotton; either very sheer and fine or coarse (like cheesecloth).

Ottoman

Ideal as an upholstery fabric; this is a firm and lustrous, horizontally ribbed, fabric, often made with a silk warp and a cotton weft.

Percale

Very fine, high-quality cotton.

Poplin

Originally made from silk and wool, but nowadays from cotton (Egyptian) and with a slightly silky finish. Poplin has a fine cross-ribbed pattern,

which is formed by using weft threads that are thicker than those of the warp threads.

Satin

A plain, closely woven silk with a smooth and lustrous finish. The wrong side of the fabric has a more matt finish. Satin is resembled by the less-expensive cotton- or wool-based fabric known as sateen.

Silk

Silk is one of the most luxurious of furnishing fabrics but not necessarily the most expensive – especially plain silks and silk mixes. It needs protection from strong sunlight and because it will show water marks it should be dry cleaned only.   **1**

Taffeta

A plain woven cloth with subtle surface ribs, traditionally made from silk. Shot-silk taffeta, where the warp and weft threads are in contrasting colours, gives the fabric the appearance of changing colour when light falls on the surface as it moves.

Tapestry

Originally hand embroidered in silk or wool, often depicting a pictorial scene. Nowadays tapestries can be created by jacquard looms.

Ticking

A strong, closely woven twill which forms a herringbone stripe, commonly known as mattress ticking. It is used for pillow cases and mattresses and usually woven with a contrasting black, red or blue stripe against an off-white background.

Tweed

A plain or twill weave from wool, often in two or more colours to create a checked pattern.

Twill

A basic weave with a diagonal grain that can be woven in any fibre.

Velvet

This is a thick, luxurious fabric with a dense pile, which is formed by either lifting the warp threads over wires and then cutting the loop

(known as cut pile) or weaving two cloths simultaneously face to face, and then slicing them apart to form two separate velvet piles. Velvet is lustrous and can be woven in silk, linen, mohair and synthetic fibres, with a different finish resulting from each.

Wool

Wool can be used as a furnishing fabric – for example, wool tartan, which is prized for its patterning; chenilles; even damask. Worsted, a combed wool, gives a strong, smooth finish.   **5**

Printed fabrics

Batik

A decorative technique for adding pattern to cloth. A design is drawn on in melted wax. The cloth is dyed, but the dye does not permeate the cloth where the wax is present. The wax is removed, leaving the pattern.

Block print

Printing using carved wooden blocks applied by hand. Major form of printing until the mid-eighteenth century.

Chintz

From the Hindu word *chitta*. Originally a painted or printed cotton cloth from India, this fabric traditionally depicts the tree of life, flowers and foliage, etc. Nowadays, it is used to describe a glazed cloth with floral printed pattern.

Paisley

Stylized curving floral or fruit forms, from patterns originating in India. The pattern can also be woven.

Toile de Jouy

Depicts light-hearted pastoral or pictorial scenes in a single colour on an off-white background. The style originated in the eighteenth century in the French town of Jouy-en-Josas.

Customizing plain fabrics

Painting

This is an inexpensive way of customizing plain fabrics with your own unique colour schemes and designs. Fabric paints or crayons are easily available from good artist's suppliers or from department stores. Emulsion, acrylic, metallic or spray paints are all equally effective and easy to use. Apply all paints in a well-ventilated area and, if spraying, it is a good idea to wear a face-mask.

To apply the paint, use a decorator's brush in whatever size is most appropriate for the line or shape you are making. Scrunched-up rags can add interesting texture. All the different techniques for applying paint - for example, spattering, stippling and stencilling - will result in markedly different effects. If you are using more than one colour, be sure to let each layer dry before the next is added.

Most types of fabrics will accept paint. The flatter the fabric – that is, the less texture it has – the easier it will be to apply the paint. Unbleached calico, canvas or other flattish cottons are perfect. However, silks and velvets provide luxurious backdrops for painting, although they require a little more attention and care. Ironing 'fixes' the paint in place.

Dyeing

There are numerous different dyestuffs and the range of colours, particularly if you mix them yourself, is unlimited. For example, subtle tones can be achieved with the liquid from boiling onion skins or walnut shells. Consult a specific manual if your enthusiasm for natural dyeing so demands.

A clever, and simple, device for giving fabrics a faded look of age is to make an infusion of tea or coffee and dip fabrics into the mixture. Subtle sepia tones can be achieved on plain fabrics, particularly muslin. Relatively inexpensive cotton or linen prints can be transformed by this method, and the technique works exceptionally well on delicately printed floral patterns. However, the effect is not permanent and will fade in due course, or with washing.

Dye, like paint, can be fixed by heat when the cloth has dried. At home, an iron provides the most effective method. Proprietary fixers can also be employed.

Dyeing with a wax resist

Hot melted wax can be used to create patterns on fabrics. Traditionally, this technique is known as 'batik'. Like paint, wax can be controlled to achieve subtle, detailed texture and pattern or, if you prefer, a looser, more abstract effect. To begin with, hot wax is painted or drawn onto a plain fabric. Use a tjanting, a tool specially designed for dribbling the wax onto the surface. When the wax has cooled down sufficiently the fabric is immersed in dye. Once dry, the wax is removed by applying a hot iron and soaking up the melted wax with a clean cloth. The area where the wax was applied will retain the ground colour.

Dyeing with wallpaper paste

Another technique, similar to dyeing with wax, is dyeing with cold-water wallpaper paste. This gives both texture and stiffness to fabric, and has added bonuses in that the paste is both inexpensive and easy to apply.

The glorious aspect of this technique is that the stiffness of the finished result can easily be altered, as the paste can be repeatedly softened and removed with water.

Spread the clean, dry fabric on a large, flat surface. Mix up the paste, which should be not too thick: roughly the consistency of jam. Using a wide wallpaper-hanging brush, apply the paste and leave it to dry. At this point, immerse the whole piece in a bath of cold-water dye. The colour will be absorbed by the paste. The fabric is slippery at this stage and, before the paste dries again, you can run a dry brush or stick across the surface to make patterns and create texture. The

fabric, still pasted, can be left to dry now, resulting in a fairly stiff, textured cloth. Alternatively, if, after drying, you immerse it again and this time remove all the paste while it is still in the water, the cloth will retain its patterned surface but be softer to the touch.

Calico or lightweight canvas is ideal for dyeing with wallpaper paste. Working with these fabrics is a little like using papier-mâché, in that you can 'sculpt' with the pasted, stiffened cloth. You could try wrapping a side-table (obviously not an antique piece!) in the wet, pasted fabric and folding and draping the fabric to get a snug fit. When the fabric dries, it will retain its shape.▷

◀◀ *Richly coloured fabrics can make a decorative scheme come alive. While the rest of the colours in this conservatory are neutral and understated, the cushions' rainbow hues create a feeling of warmth and informality.*

◀ *Customizing plain fabrics with paint allows a great deal of scope for creativity. The designs embellishing this stone-coloured bed-linen resemble charcoal sketches or plasterwork mouldings, and create an unusual* trompe-l'oeil *effect.*

Printing

To achieve a more controlled pattern on fabric, it is better to print, using a linocut or stamp. Simple borders can be run around the edge of a fabric using this quick and easy method and it can be cleverly utilized for small items like cushion covers.

Obviously, the more professional you want your finish to be, the more likely you are to need proper tools; there are special lino-cutting tools, for example. But whether you use a potato, lino or a sponge, the areas that you cut out will not take up printing ink.

A version of this method uses washing-up sponges – the sort that are rectangular and have a stiff scouring base. Use a felt-tip pen to mark up a grid on the soft side of the sponge. Divide it into squares with 6mm (¼in) gutters between the squares. Cut along the lines and hollow out the channels.

Squeeze acrylic paint onto a plate and thin it with water to the consistency of single cream. Alternatively, use fabric paints. Press the cut face of the sponge into the paint. Do not make it so thin and wet that it drips.

Ensure that your fabric is stretched out flat, either using weights or, preferably, pinning it to a board. Then, carefully and lightly, press the sponge onto the surface of the fabric and you will achieve a kind of mosaic pattern. You may want to test the technique first on a piece of paper to ensure that you have the paint at the correct consistency and so that you can decide how much paint you actually need on the sponge – be careful not to smudge prints you have already made as you print more.

You can make a chequerboard pattern using two sponge 'tiles' and two colours. Print one colour first, filling in the missing squares with the other only when it is dry.

Combining fabrics

This is the fabric equivalent of 'distressed' paint finishes! By breaking down and re-assembling related or contrasting fabrics in one item – a throw or bed hanging, perhaps – you can create both unexpected and wonderful combinations and a distinctly original 'fabric'. The idea extends and refines the idea of the patchwork quilt. As in all decoration, however, there has to be a balance: the two, three or many more different fabrics that work pleasingly together must result in a piece that is more than just the sum of its parts.

Pile more than half a dozen fabrics together on a table and you will see some kind of link. Maybe it is simply a red line from a tartan which jumps to a silk damask of the same hue, or the creaminess of old bleached linen against a rough jute which in

▶ These cushions would have been fairly anonymous without their embroidered daisy details and deliberately rough-and-ready stitching. Customizing soft furnishings can lift them out of the ordinary. It is also cost-effective, enabling you to put scraps of old dress material and leftover snippets of upholstery fabric to good use.

Printing fabric

1 Mark a grid with felt pen on the sponge's soft face; cut channels along the lines to make a pad of squares.

2 Squeeze paint onto plate; dilute with water to single-cream consistency; press cut face of sponge into paint.

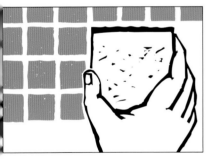

3 Test technique on paper to avoid smudging and drips; then press sponge carefully and lightly onto flat fabric.

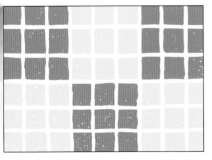

4 Print all the first colour of a chequerboard effect and allow to dry before filling in second-colour squares.

▲ *These fabrics have been painted and resist-dyed in colours of jewel-like intensity. Their inspiration ranges from batik fabrics and Indian saris to the boldly striped walls and furnishings of Regency salons. Simple trimmings can enhance soft-furnishing fabrics still further; here, a gold-braid edging gives the shimmering sapphire-coloured cushion an ornate finish.*

turn lies against a cream–and–black striped cotton. Occasionally, a cornucopia of pink, lime green, purple and orange, although not to everyone's taste, just simply works.

If the colour links in some way, you can mix your fabrics. Equally, mix different textures – silk, poplin, canvas, damask and velvet, for example.

It is also interesting to use fabrics of varying weights together in one piece: such as thin muslin and velvet, or hessian and silk. You then have a fabric that moves in a different way, and demands to be hung or displayed more cleverly, or suggests new uses.

Stitching small circles of frayed coloured cloth randomly across the surface of another fabric – like mattress tufts – is another exciting method of customizing; as is stitching itself, which can transform fabric by adding colour and texture.

Work out the quantity of fabric you wish to use fairly carefully, allowing extra for hemming, etc. The keys to the success of the final piece are both planning and accurate cutting. Fabrics for piping should be cut on the bias (the cross of the fabric) and therefore more fabric is required. Use faint pencil lines as a cutting guide.

Seating

Seating is all about comfort and style – and balancing the right amount of both. How this is achieved will depend on where in the house, garden or office the seating is to be and, more crucially, the part it is to play. Whether we are working at a desk or flopping down at the end of a busy day, comfort is paramount. A set of chairs able to withstand day-to-day use at family mealtimes will need a more practical design than the more stylish dining-room chairs used only on highdays and holidays.

It does not trouble us if wooden furniture for the garden is allowed to mellow and take on a rough, weathered patina, but we treat an antique mahogany dining chair with tender loving care, polishing it reverently and making sure it receives no damage.

Different rooms and living spaces will, naturally, have varying styles of seating. Individual items are far more likely to make an impact – and be chosen for that purpose – in areas where they can be surrounded by considerable space. For example, an intricately carved old church pew or a tall, elegant wing armchair, whose upholstered sections are each covered in different fabrics, could be viewed as a decorative object when placed individually, and would provide a strong focal point for an interior. Their comfort appeal would be secondary to their looks.

Specific items will undoubtedly influence the addition of others. Selection should, though, be based on what you like and feel good about rather than on trying to 'match' a set of furniture. In areas such as living rooms, where several items of seating often mingle together, overall cohesion is important, although individual items may clash dramatically. This is where balance is essential.

The uses of fabric

Fabric can be used to link or group seating elements together with covers, throws or cushions. By choosing one colour, such as oatmeal, and covering all seating in that colour, whether upholstered armchairs, sofas or dining-chair seats, an interior is created that is instantly calming and uncluttered. However, it would be dramatically livened up if other coloured fabrics or other surfaces – wood, metal, leather, or glass, for example – were allowed in. A riot of different patterns on printed or woven fabrics can coexist provided that there is a strong colour link running through them and given that there are also areas of calm, such as plain walls and floors, to anchor them.

In addition, fabric appeals to our tactile sense, creating a feeling of warmth and comfort. More than any other material, it completely transforms a surface. By introducing a cushion on a painted wooden

◀ *A large kilim anchors the seating area in this wonderfully lively and colourful room. The sofa, upholstered in a plain cream fabric, offsets the riot of colour going on around it. The alcove, with a built-in covered seat, provides a place to escape, while multicoloured cushions occupy every available surface.*

▲ *Furniture has been carefully placed to fill out – but not clutter – this area in a large converted warehouse. The day-bed, sited in the middle of the room rather than predictably hugging a wall, doubles as seating. The lamp next to the sofa and the large floor rug by the day-bed help to mark out the space.*

window seat or a chunky wool throw over the back of a plain sofa, you can change the style and character of seating surfaces – and the room – with relative ease.

Designing your seating

How seating is arranged in a room or living space is pivotal to the success of the room, from both practical and style viewpoints. In small or awkward spaces such as those under stairs, housing a free-standing piece of seating furniture would be difficult, but a built-in wooden box structure covered with loose cushions would make good use of this kind of space, transforming it into a wonderful 'cubbyhole' seating area for quiet reading. Give the box seat a lid and, of course, you have storage space too!

Long, narrow living rooms need careful planning, with groups of items strategically placed so that the entire room can be used, especially if different activities have to take place in the same space. If the entire living space is one room – whether in a vast warehouse or a more modest abode – an element of flexibility is important. Mix smaller items such as stools and side chairs with larger, more imposing pieces. Combine period-inspired furniture with a modern piece or a simple item found in a junk shop. Don't be intimidated at the thought of larger items, such as sofas or benches, being positioned in the middle of the floor. Set chairs at interesting diagonals to 'break up' space. And if the key to your space is a good desk, a chair and a computer, then put them centre stage!

Basic cushions

Cushions can be roughly divided into two types: those that fit a given space and those that lead a more nomadic existence – the ubiquitous scatter cushion. The former category, usually 'box' cushions, are made to a specific size, dictated by the space between the arms and back of a sofa or chair, or the dimensions of a flat wooden bench top or window seat. The latter group can be of all shapes and sizes and their domain is infinitely varied. These padded, plumped discs and squares of piped, fringed and braided colour can sometimes, surprisingly, be the single element that gives balance and focus to a room or piece of furniture. The eye darts about in a room, settling on pattern, texture and colour, so a small cushion or pile of cushions can attract and become a link between otherwise unrelated items.

Mixing different surfaces, materials and textiles in one space is exciting. For example, adding a pair of square cushions in a fake leopard skin against a cool backdrop of neutral off-white and beige linen inspires a flight of fantasy that could make bringing ornate gilt and black lacquer furniture into the room acceptable, whereas before it might otherwise have been rejected. Against the same backdrop, imagine a pile of cushions made of rich tapestries, old tangled fringes and near-faded silks in a warm mix of red, ochre and terracotta, and you have a completely different atmosphere.

Cushion styles

Basic square, rectangular or round cushion covers have two sides of fabric, stitched together. The opening for the cushion pad can be fastened by simple slip stitches or by way of a zip, buttons or ties (see pages 38–39, 45–47). The two sides need not be of the same fabric – each side could be a combination of fabrics joined before the cushion cover is constructed. Piping or decorative cord can add definition, while braids, fringes and buttons lend texture. Cushion covers can be made so that the stitching line hugs the edge of the pad and is surrounded by a border (like an Oxford pillow case). The border, usually about 5cm (2in) wide, might be in the same fabric as the cushion, or in a contrast.

For a smart tailored look, combine crisp white linen for the main part of the cushion with a fine cotton shirting in a white and coloured stripe for a piping detail, and for the surrounding border use a check of hound's-or dog's-tooth. Use the same three fabrics on other cushions in the same group but switch the focus. Borders can be extended, and for a rectangular cushion, like a bed pillow, a large border at the open end secured by buttons is particularly smart.

For a totally different style, take as your inspiration the rich contrast between a wool blanket and the silky band that borders it

▶ *This beautiful wooden bench needs only the simplest of decoration. A box cushion covering the upholstered base offers softer seating, and a row of substantial square cushions in cool, creamy white fabric makes a simple, uncluttered and stylish addition to the piece as well as providing further comfort.*

and make a cover that combines smart wool suiting with a surround of brightly coloured silk. Alternatively, mix a multitude of stripes or checks or even different scale floral patterns – printed or woven – but bear in mind that a colour link should bind them. One of the attractive aspects of making cushion covers is that they take only a small amount of fabric and are therefore relatively inexpensive decorative touches.

Making a square cushion cover

To make a plain, square cushion cover without piping, first decide on the finished cushion size. Cut two squares of fabric to the size of the cushion plus a 1.5cm (⅝in) seam allowance all around. With right sides facing and raw edges aligned, pin and tack the two pieces together, then remove the pins. Working a few reverse stitches at each end of the seam, machine stitch around the edge, leaving an opening along one side for turning

and inserting the cushion. Remove the tacking, trim the seam allowances and clip the corners to reduce bulk, leaving a gap of approximately 6mm (¼in) to avoid fraying. Press the seams.

Turn the cover right side out through the opening and push out the corners so that they are sharp. Press the cover and then insert the cushion. Finally, turn under the seam allowances along the opening, pin and slip stitch closed.

Making a round cushion cover

If made without a band between the top and bottom of the cushion, round cushions are just two circular fabric pieces sewn together with or without a line of piping between the two. Cord or a small shallow fringe can be hand sewn around the finished cushion. For variety, cut two halves of different, contrasting fabrics for each side. Join them together and then proceed as if for one piece. ▷

Making a square cushion

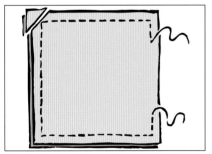

1 With right sides facing, stitch the back and front together, leaving an opening. Trim corners diagonally.

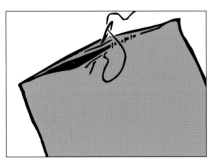

2 Press the seams open. Turn the cover right side out, insert the cushion and slip stitch the opening closed.

▲ Layer upon layer of simple cushions form a soft backing for a day-bed. A pile of the same cushions, secured with tied tabs, are strategically positioned to form the arms of the bed. A mixture of warm terracotta, charcoal and ochre fabrics, offset by the occasional black-and-white stripe, makes a bold combination.

To make a paper pattern for the cushion cover, draw around a suitably sized object such as a large plate, then add a 1.5cm (⅝in) seam allowance all around. Alternatively, cut a paper square with dimensions matching the diameter of the required finished circle plus extra for seam allowances. Fold the square into quarters and lay it on a flat surface. Tie a pencil onto the end of a length of string, then pin the other end of the string to the centre of the folded square so that the string between the pencil and the pin measures the radius of the required circle, plus a 1.5cm (⅝in) seam allowance. Draw a quarter-circle arc on the paper and cut out.

Open out the paper circle and, using this as your pattern, cut out one fabric piece for the front of the cover and one for the back. Pin and tack the two pieces together, with right sides facing and raw edges aligned. Remove the pins. Working a few reverse stitches at each end of the seam, machine stitch around the cover, leaving an opening for turning and for inserting the cushion. Remove the tacking, then trim and notch the seam allowance to reduce bulk. Press the seam open. Turn the cover right side out and press again, turning the seam allowances to the wrong side along the opening. Insert the cushion. Pin and stitch the opening closed.

Tie-on cushions

Square or round cushions that are to be used as seat pads sometimes need anchoring to a wooden or wicker chair or bench so that they don't slip off. Ties looped around the back of the frame are the answer.

Simple covers for seat pads can be made in the same way as a basic cushion cover but with a pair of ties stitched into the back edge of the cushion between the two pieces of fabric. Tie-on cushions may be made square or round, and with or without piping. Alternatively, they can be made as flattish box cushions where the welt or gusset would only be 5cm (2in) or less (see pages 40–41).

The ties can serve a decorative as well as a functional purpose. For example, unyielding wooden chairs, such as old school desk chairs, benefit by tying a cushion onto the seat to add comfort and colour.

▲ *Made to fit the seats of these metal-framed chairs, these round cushions add style as well as comfort. The two on the chair in the foreground have both been made deeper by means of a band or gusset, but the one leaning against the back of the other chair consists of just two circles of fabric joined together with piping.*

Making a round cushion

1 To make a paper pattern, fold a square of paper into quarters, draw a quarter-circle and cut out.

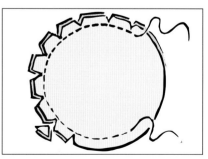

2 Cut two fabric circles. Stitch as for the square cushion (see page 37), but notch the seam allowance.

Making a tie-on cushion cover

To make the ties, cut strips of fabric in either the same or a contrasting fabric (the two fabrics should be the same composition and weight) to a length that will allow for a reasonable knot or bow around the back of the chair frame. The width of the finished tie should be no more than about 3cm (1¼in). Cut the fabric to twice the width of the finished tie, plus a hem allowance of 12mm (½in) on each side and at each short end.

Fold the fabric strip in half lengthways, right sides together, and press. Machine stitch, 12mm (½in) from the raw edge, across one short end and all along the length of the strip. Turn the tube right side out with the aid of a knitting needle or narrow ruler, pushing through from the stitched short end. Alternatively, the tie can be made by top stitching the edges together. To do this, first press the 12mm (½in) seam allowances to the wrong side along both long edges and one short end. Then fold the strip in half lengthways with the wrong sides together, and machine stitch close to the aligned folded edges. Set the finished ties aside.

Next, make a paper pattern to the required finished size and shape of the cushion cover, plus a 1.5cm (⅝in) seam allowance all around. Using this pattern, cut out the top and bottom of the cushion cover. Mark the chair leg (or chair back) positions on the bottom section of the cover, and pin two finished ties to each of the marked positions, with the short raw edges aligned with

the raw edges of the cover piece and the ties lying on the centre of the piece. Pin the top of the cushion to the bottom, with right sides together and raw edges aligned. Tack, catching in the ends of the ties in the seam. Remove the pins. Machine stitch around the edge, leaving an opening for turning and for inserting the cushion. Remove the tacking, trim, clip and notch the seam allowance to avoid bulk. Press the seam open. Turn the cover right side out and press. Insert the cushion. Pin and slip stitch the opening closed, as for the square cushion.

Alternative cushion ideas

Cushion covers can be interchanged to suit the mood of the interior. One cover inside another, with the outer one with contrasting ties, is a less formal, more fun approach and great for children's rooms. Big square cushions look good with button fastenings. Choose plain, unfussy buttons for matt fabrics such as cotton tickings, linens or ging-

hams, delicate little mother-of-pearl buttons for finer fabrics and big, bold, brassy ones for heavy brocades, silks or damasks.

Stitching applied to the surface of plain fabrics lends texture and pattern. Embroidery stitches can be used to great effect. Create spidery latticework, a riot of multicoloured dots or crosses or copy formal motifs. Appliqué stars or other shapes using a bold blanket stitch. Cut out images from printed fabrics, such as farm animals, in bold silhouettes for children's rooms, and stitch them onto plain fabrics.

Try constructing a cushion cover from a knitted square. Use creamy, soft string – the kind you find in a kitchen drawer or that ties parcels. Combine with chunky cotton cord in place of piping and hand sew the opening or use buttons. In bathrooms, or for outside in the summer when all you want is to relax with a pillow beneath your head, use waterproof canvas, and foam instead of feathers, for easy cleaning.

Making a tie-on cushion

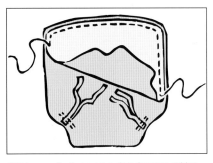

1 Make up as for the square cushion (see page 37) but stitch the ties into the seam allowance.

◄ *Seat cushions on an intriguingly designed sofa and chairs are covered with bright citrus fabrics. Each cover has a row of fabric tabs attached to the cover opening which are tied together, with the knots adding a decorative finish to the back of the cushions.*

Box cushions

When a cushion is really a seat and is required to take on a more practical and, consequently, sturdier role, its shape is more like a box than a flat pad. The cover for it, which has a gusset or welt between the upper and lower sections, has six sides, like a box. A box cushion should be fairly solid so that the required shape is kept. It can be filled with feather and down or, for a firmer base, it can be cut from foam with a layer of wadding around it.

Box cushions are most usually seen on the seat of an upholstered armchair, or two or three may be used snugly side by side on the base of a sofa.

An essential part of a Bergère chair, which does not have other upholstered sections, is the box cushion which sits on the flat base. Wooden chairs, where a loose seat pad of some kind is required for comfort, also rely on a sturdy box cushion.

Depending on the design of the chair or sofa, there may also be a box cushion to lean against, made in the same way but positioned roughly at right angles to the base cushion.

Making a box cushion cover

To make your box cushion cover, begin by cutting two pieces of material the same size as the top and bottom of the pad, adding 1.5cm (⅝in) all around for a seam allowance.

The welt is made up of five pieces. Cut one piece to fit the front of the welt, allowing for a seam allowance all around. Then cut two pieces long enough to fit across the back of the welt, plus 5cm (2in) extra at each end so that the back welt will extend around the two back corners, again adding a seam allowance all around each piece. Lastly, cut one welt piece for each side of the cushion to fit between the front and back welts.

Insert the zip between the two back welt pieces (see page 47). With right sides facing, now pin and stitch the gusset pieces together, leaving 1.5cm (⅝in) open at each end of the two front seams. Press the seams open. If you are using piping, stitch it to the top and bottom pieces (see pages 48–49). Next, pin and tack the welt to the bottom piece, with right sides together and front corners matching. Clip the seam allowance

▲ *A simple wooden structure creates a clever seating area and transforms an otherwise featureless window space. Thick, heavy cushions, with their edges rolled rather than piped, align to form a padded, bench-like seat against the three walls. Rather like mattresses, the cushions are buttoned to prevent the covers moving.*

▶ *Piped edgings give shape and definition to soft furnishings, and here they are used to great effect in highlighting the deliberately overstuffed box cushion seat of this ample Victorian wing chair. The use of the same russet and gold damask for both the piping and cover adds a simple touch of refinement.*

on the welt at each of the two back corners. Remove the pins and stitch into place. Open the zip and attach the welt to the top piece in the same way. Trim the seam allowances and corners and press. Turn right side out through the zip and press.

Decorative effects for box cushions

This type of cushion looks best with piping or cord added along the seams between the top, the base sections and the welt. This emphasizes the distinctive box shape of the cushion, but it can also be a decorative feature, particularly if it is made in a fabric contrasting with the main fabric.

The art of buttoning, although best left to the professional upholsterer, can give the surface of the cushion both texture and a rich, almost quilted look. Secure on either side of the cushion with a linking cord or strong thread pulled right through the cushion and pad; buttons or pompoms will cause the top of the cushion to undulate, like a bed mattress. Use fabric-covered buttons or, for a real sense of luxury, small pompons (little tufts of cotton, wool or silk) or small circles or squares of fabric.

To brighten up a rather plain club armchair, choose four different coloured fabrics from the same family: for example, a striped velvet in a peacock blue, a plain dark navy velvet, a deep scarlet and one in tangerine. With the main part of the chair upholstered in a combination of the different fabrics – you might have the tangerine on one arm and the red on the other with the navy blue between – make up the box cushion with each visible facet in a different colour.

Other ideas for box cushions

Long, thin box cushions, essentially with a narrow welt, make the top of a wooden box or bench a comfortable seat. Simply constructed wooden boxes with lids make excellent storage spaces and can double up as seats around an informal kitchen table. Box cushions can also be shaped to fit a window seat. Measure carefully and cut a template from newspaper to ensure that the cushion fits neatly, as sometimes, especially in old houses, the shape may not be symmetrical.

Making a box cushion cover

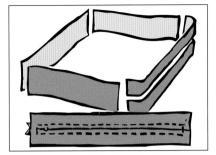

1 Cut out the top and bottom cover pieces and the five welt pieces. Insert the zip between the back welt pieces.

2 Stitch the welt strips together, leaving 1.5cm (⅝in) open at each end of the front seams. Check the fit.

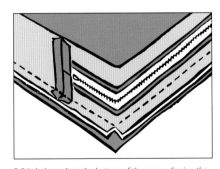

3 Stitch the welt to the bottom of the cover, clipping the welt seam allowance at the two back corners.

4 Open the zip. Stitch the welt to the top of the cover. Trim the corners diagonally and turn right side out.

Bolster cushions

As their name suggests, bolster cushions offer a means of support for other cushions or pillows. Stuffed with feathers or other fillings, they are long or short rolls that lie along the end or sides of a day-bed or on certain types of sofa. On bench sofas, with one long mattress-type seat cushion, it would not be unusual to see a short bolster at each end.

Open-ended bolster covers

In a room that requires the bed to double up as a sofa by day, an open-ended bolster cover can store rolled bedding quite neatly. A quick knot in the fabric at each end of the cover keeps everything in place. Alternatively, a length of tied cord or a specially made band with a button and buttonhole would do just as well to close the cover, and would add a note of sophistication.

For this type of versatile cover, a long cylinder of fabric is all that is needed. It should be longer than the rolled duvet that will be inside it. The surplus fabric at each end, once tied or secured, can fall attractively over the edges of the bed. The width of the cover should be the same as the circumference of the rolled stuffing. Long fabric ties, sewn to the ends of the cover, secure them.

Closed-end bolster covers

The simplest way to make a bolster cover with closed ends is to sew a tube of fabric and gather each end neatly together so that it meets in the centre of the end like a drawstring bag. On this type of cover, the shape

▲ This sofa is given a formal, symmetrical appearance with two bolsters lined up across its back and all its elements made from the same fabric. In pleasingly relaxed contrast, however, are the loose tailored covers and the use of different finishes at either end of the bolsters – flat against the inside arms but bunched and tied in the middle.

Making a basic bolster cover

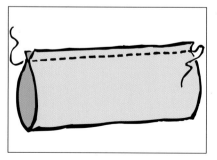

1 Cut the bolster cover piece long enough to exceed the ends and stitch the two long sides together to form a tube.

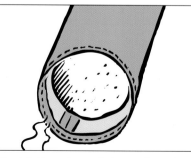

2 Turn right side out, then turn in the seam allowances at each end. Make a row of gathering stitches along the fold.

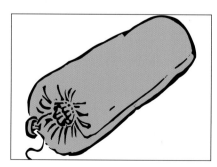

3 Gather the ends of the cover. Stitch a large button or a pompon over each gathered centre.

Making a fitted bolster cover

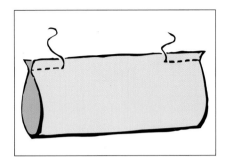

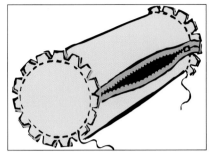

1 Cut the main cover piece and stitch together to form a tube, leaving a gap for the zip. Press the seam open.

2 Insert the zip. Stitch on the circular ends. Notch the seam allowances and press. Turn right side out.

of the bolster can be defined by adding strips of contrasting fabric to the main fabric at each end which, when the ends of the cover are drawn together, appear as attractive concentric circles. Ribbons can create a similar effect but need to be applied to the fabric – that is, sewn onto the surface like appliqué.

Making a basic bolster cover

To determine the length of the cover piece, add the length of the bolster to the diameter of the end, plus a 2cm (¾in) seam allowance at each end. For the width, add 3cm (1¼in) for the two seam allowances to the circumference of the bolster. Cut a piece of fabric to this size. Fold it in half lengthways, with right sides together and raw edges aligned, and pin. Machine stitch 1.5cm (⅝in) from the raw edge. (If a zip is required, leave a gap in this seam and insert the zip at this stage.) Press the seam open. Turn the cover right side out. Turn 2cm (¾in) to the wrong side at each end and press. Using a strong thread doubled, hand stitch a line of running stitches close to the folded edge at each end. Then insert the bolster into the centre of the fabric tube. Gather the ends of the cover, tying the thread ends together and securing them inside the centre of the gathers.

Adding piping to a bolster cover

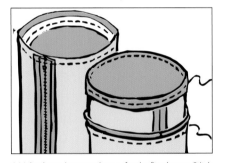

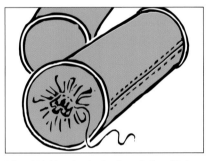

1 Make the main cover piece as for the fitted cover. Stitch the piping to the ends, then add an extra strip of fabric.

2 Turn right side out and gather the ends. For a fitted cover, simply attach the piping before the circular end.

▲ *Some clever examples of the ways in which bolster covers can be finished off. While a simple, flat end is very functional, a random gathering of surplus fabric at each end of a rolled-up cylinder can be tied into bunches with a band of ribbon. This is one of the simplest and most effective of finishing techniques, requiring no sewing.*

Fitted bolster covers

For a more tailored look, the bolster end can be a separately inserted circular piece of fabric. The centre of the circle can be further embellished with a whirl of cord, a dangling key tassel, a brass or chrome ring or a button.

Making a fitted bolster cover

Cut the main cover piece as long as the bolster and as wide as the circumference of the bolster plus a 1.5cm (⅝in) seam allowance all around. Fold in half lengthways, with right sides together and raw edges aligned, and pin. Tack and then machine stitch, leaving a gap for the zip. Press the seam open. Turn the cover right side out and insert the zip (see page 47). Open the zip and turn the tube wrong side out. Pin, tack and stitch the circular ends to the tube. Trim and notch the seam allowances. Press the seams open and then turn the cover right side out.

Adding piping to the ends

To attach piping around the circular ends of the bolster, cut and stitch the main cover piece as for a fitted bolster cover. Stitch the piping to the right side of the ends. On a basic bolster cover, add an extra tube of fabric at each end that is long enough to cover the end and turn the cover right side out. Gather the ends as for the basic cover. On a fitted cover, stitch on the circular ends after attaching the piping to the main piece.

Decorative effects for the bolsters

For a more sophisticated bolster, combine fabrics and cord in one cover. For a touch of flamboyance, mix fake leopard skin, dramatic ink-blue silk and a shiny gold cord and key tassel. Hand-stitched braid or other passementerie go well with all kinds of fabric: a rough hessian looks surprisingly good with an elegantly woven trim, for example.

Directory of fastenings and trimmings

There is a wide range of decorative trimmings available for use on cushion covers, tablecloths, place mats and bed-linen. They can be chosen in a contrasting colour, pattern or texture to add a bold foil to soft furnishings or can be in a plain, matching colour to create a subtle but striking detail.

Fastenings on your cushion covers, loose covers or pillow cases serve a practical purpose but can also be a design focus, as becomes obvious with the use of ties or bold buttons.

Edgings

Bias binding

Bias binding is a strip of fabric, cut on the bias (diagonally across the grain) and used for enclosing piping cord or for covering raw edges – for example, around the edges of place mats.

Bias binding can be handmade from any lightweight fabric, patterned, plain or striped. It can also be bought ready-made in various widths and in a range of solid colours.

Braid

Decorative braid is a narrow, woven strip, often hand-worked, with a raised texture and fancy patterning. It can be applied to fabric to edge cushions, or sewn onto loose or fitted covers to emphasize colour or shape. Often it is used to decorate lampshades.

Two especially effective types of braid are gimp, which is a braided woven trim shaped like a close, continuous 'S', and picot braid, which is a ribbed trimming.

Cords and piping

Cords and piping are used to edge cushions, covers and upholstery and are often positioned to hide seams.

Ready-made decorative cords are usually made from twisted strands of silk, cotton, jute, wool, etc. Cord comes in varying thicknesses and can be single or multicoloured. Some cord comes with a flange for inserting between the fabric layers.

Piping is a fabric-covered cord. It can be bought ready-made or can be handmade by covering a filler cord with a narrow strip of fabric (see pages 48–49). Double-piping is a double row of covered cord (or piping) also used to edge upholstery.   **3**

Fringes

Fringe is a loose-hanging trim usually made from wool, silk or cotton. It can be fine or thick, and is often encrusted with knots or beads for added decoration. Bullion fringing is a more elaborate, thick twisted fringe, often containing gold or metallic threads.

Other trims

Rosettes

These small, circular, woven decorations can be stitched to the surface of covers on the front arms of chairs or sofas. They imitate the shape of a rose and can often be quite ornate.

Studs

Metal or brass upholstery studs can be either flat or dome-headed and are nailed into the edges of upholstered chairs, footstools and sofas, particularly Chesterfield sofas, where they form an integral part of the style. They hold the fabric in place, act as a decorative trim or help to conceal raw edges. Some can be quite decorative, with the surfaces 'antiqued' or carved.   **4**

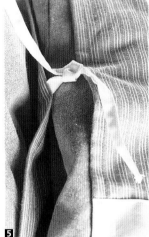

5

4

Tapestry strips

Firm, narrow woven bands, imitating hand-stitched tapestry, the strips are applied to the edges of covers or cushions or embellish chair and sofa seats. Designs are usually traditional and often echo architectural mouldings.

Tassels

These dangling decorative trims are made of bunched yarn or cord. They are either attached to rope (for example, for looping around sofa ends or holding back curtains) or are joined to small rosettes (key tassels) for attaching to keys on doors or drawers. **1**

Fastenings

Buttons

Available in any number of shapes and sizes and made from brass, glass, bone or mother-of-pearl, to name but a few materials. Buttons and buttonholes are used to fasten all kinds of edges on soft furnishings. Buttons (without buttonholes) can be used to make unusual decorative patterns. **2**

Eyelets

Metal eyelet kits come with a punch and dye to cut holes in fabric and then to secure a brass or chrome ring to hold together the raw edges of the hole. Eyelets are corded or roped together to join two edges of fabric.

Fabric ties and ribbons

Silk, cotton or synthetic ribbons and handmade fabric ties have many uses in furnishings. They can be tied in bows to hold two open edges together or can simply be tied or knotted to edges for decoration. **5**

Press studs

A useful fastening device, but one intended to be hidden, press studs are small metal fasteners that are stitched to either side of an opening and then clipped shut to close the opening. They can be used to secure cushions.

Velcro fastening

Much disliked by traditionalists, Velcro (also known as 'touch-and-close' or 'hook and loop' fastening) is a quick and simple method of holding fabric in place. It consists of two pieces of nylon tape, one with a soft, furry, looped surface and the other with a rougher surface which is actually made up of rows of tiny hooks. When the two tapes are pressed together the hooks 'link' with the soft surface and a fairly strong bond results. The tapes are sewn to the edges of the fabric – for example, the underside of the open edges of a duvet cover. Velcro comes in a variety of widths and colours and can be sewn to fabric or stuck to a harder surface.

Zippers

The most practical of fastenings, a zip consists of two fabric tapes edged with metal teeth or a plastic coil. The teeth or coils interlock when the zip head is pulled between the two halves of the zip. Usually hidden from view behind the fabric, zips are inserted in cushion covers and loose covers so that they can be easily removed for cleaning.

Simple fastenings and zips

▲ *Cushions are marvellous furnishing tools – nothing can more easily transform a space. They can be made in all shapes and sizes and from various fabrics. The cushions above are all of different shapes but are linked into a Chinese-porcelain theme of blue and white to complement other objects in the room.*

cushion (see page 37), but allow for a hem allowance of 7.5cm (3in) along the opening edge of each piece.

Pin a double hem in place along the opening edge on each piece by turning 2.5cm (1in) to the wrong side twice. Slip stitch or machine stitch the hem and then press. With the right sides facing, machine stitch the two cushion pieces together along the other three sides. Then at each end of the opening edge, stitch 5cm (2in) close to the double hem to strengthen the sides.

Sew Velcro spots, single press studs or even a strip of press studs along each side of the opening on the double hem in corresponding positions. Trim the seam allowances of the cushion and clip the two outside corners diagonally to reduce the bulk.

Turn the cover right side out and press. Insert the cushion pad and fasten the Velcro, studs or strips together. When closed, the fastenings should not be visible.

Simple fastenings

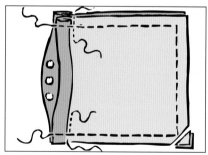

1 Attach Velcro spots or press studs to the double hems along the opening edge of the cover.

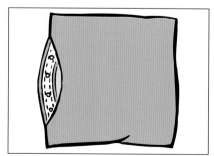

2 Attach a strip of press studs in the same way. The fastenings will be invisible on the right side.

Duvet covers, cushion covers and loose covers that require frequent washing will all require fastenings that are hard-wearing and practical. Velcro, press studs and zips meet these requirements and are the most frequently used fastenings. They are easy to conceal so that they do not detract from the main effect of the furnishing.

Velcro fastenings

Unlike other fastenings for fabrics Velcro fastenings can also be used to attach fabrics to a solid surface. For instance, they could be used to attach removable fabric panels to a room screen or to attach a valance to a wooden bed frame. In these instances and for openings that may be strained, such as duvet covers and box cushions, it is best to attach

strips of Velcro fastening. For smaller openings that do not need to be so hard-wearing, such as small scatter-cushion covers, Velcro spots are more suitable.

Press studs

Straightforward to attach, press studs work well along the inside edge of a cushion or duvet cover opening. They can be bought as single fastenings or already attached to a fabric strip. A strip of press studs is ideal for the opening of a cushion or duvet cover.

Attaching simple fastenings to a cushion cover

To make a cushion cover to be closed with Velcro spot fastenings or press studs, first cut two pieces of fabric as for a basic square

Zips

Zips can be bought to an individual size or as one continuous strip of uncut teeth. The latter is used off the reel as required and individually bought zip heads are applied to it. Choose a zip colour that suits the item it is to be attached to.

Zips can be inserted and neatly concealed in the seam of a cushion cover or duvet cover. On a square scatter cushion the zip can either be inserted in the seam at the base of the cushion or in a centre seam on the cover back, as for a round cushion.

Inserting a zip in a cushion's side seam

Cut two pieces of fabric as for a basic square cushion cover (see page 37). With right sides facing, stitch the two pieces together for 5cm (2in) at each end of the opening edge, leaving an opening for the zip. Tack the opening together along the seam line and

press the seam open. Pin and tack the zip along the seam line, with the right side of the zip facing the wrong side of the seam. Stitch around the zip (using the zipper foot on the machine) from the right side close to the tacking. Remove the tacking.

Open the zip. Then, with right sides facing, pin, tack and stitch the remaining three sides together. Remove the tacking. Trim the seam allowances, clip the corners diagonally and press the seam open. Turn the cover right side out and press again.

Inserting a zip in a cushion's back

Cut out the front of the cover as for a basic square cushion cover (see page 37). Cut another piece 3cm (1¼in) wider than the first (to allow extra for the zip seam), then cut it in half widthways.

With right sides facing, stitch the two back pieces together for 5cm (2in) at each end of the opening edge, leaving an opening

for the zip. Tack the opening together along the seam line and press the seam open. Insert the zip as for the zip in a side seam.

Open the zip and, with right sides together, pin, tack and stitch the back of the cover to the front and complete as for the zip in a side seam.

Inserting a zip in a round cushion

Make a paper pattern as for a basic round cushion cover (see page 38). Cut out the cover front using the pattern. Then cut straight across the paper pattern one third of the way from one edge. Using the two paper pieces, cut out the two pieces for the cover back, adding a seam allowance along each opening edge.

Stitch the two back pieces together and insert the zip as for the zip on a cover back (see above). Then join the back to the front with right sides together. Notch the seam allowance, turn right side out and press.

Cushion side seam

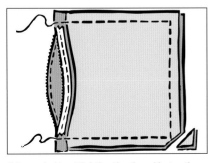

1 Stitch cover pieces together along one edge, leaving an opening for zip. Tack opening together and insert zip.

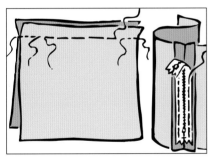

2 Remove tacking. Stitch the other three sides together. Trim and turn the cover right side out through the zip.

Cushion back

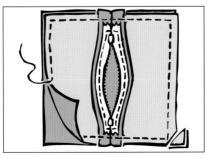

1 Stitch the back pieces together, leaving an opening. Tack opening together, press seam open and insert zip.

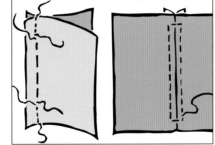

2 Remove tacking. With zip open, stitch the back to the front. Trim and turn the cover right side out.

Round cushion

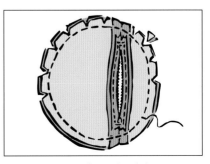

1 Using a paper pattern, cut one piece for cover front. Cut two pieces for back and insert zip in back seam.

2 Stitch the back to the front and notch the seam allowance. Turn the cover right side out through the zip.

Piping and trims

▶ Piping can add decoration and definition to a piece of furniture or a cushion. It also serves to strengthen the seams of structured items. Here, the piping emphasizes a probably unintentional contrast between the formal primness of the cream-upholstered chair and the faded old-gold velvet cover.

Nothing finishes off upholstery and soft furnishings better than edging. Using either piping, fringing, tassels or cord – available in a huge range of materials, colours and textures – creates a very professional touch and adds interest and style.

Piping

Piping is a means of adding decoration and definition to items such as a cushion, an upholstered chair or a duvet cover. It can be made in the same fabric as the main piece to which it is attached (called self-piping) or it can be made from a contrasting fabric to highlight shape or add texture.

Piping is made by enclosing a line of cord in a narrow strip of fabric. The covered cord is then inserted between two layers of fabric and stitched, leaving the piped strip visible along the seam on the right side. The piping filler cord itself is made of twisted strands of (usually) cotton, bleached or unbleached. It

Piping a cushion cover

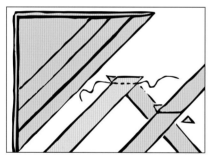

1 Cut the fabric strips to cover the piping on the bias. Join the strips end to end on the straight grain and trim.

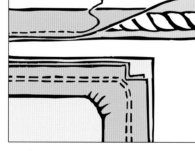

2 Stitch the strip around the cord, using a zipper foot. Stitch the piping to the cover front, snipping the corners.

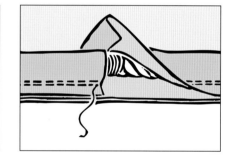

3 Trim the cord so that the ends butt together. Turn in one end of the fabric cover and lap it over the other end.

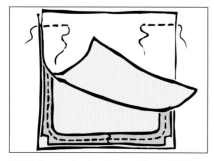

4 Stitch the cover together along one side, sandwiching the piping between the layers and leaving an opening.

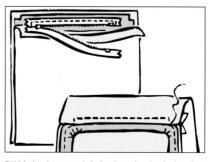

5 With the zip open, stitch the zip to the piped edge, then close it and stitch it from the front to the other edge.

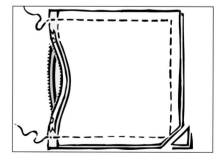

6 Open the zip and stitch the other three sides of the cover together. Trim and turn right side out.

comes in a variety of thicknesses, known by a number: 1, 2, etc. It is best to use pre-shrunk cord for anything that will later be laundered or dry-cleaned.

The strips of fabric used to cover the cord are generally cut on the bias (cross) of the fabric to give it more flexibility for easing around corners and curves. However, this is not essential. It may be that the pattern of the fabric is such that you want to cut across the width or length of the fabric.

Piping a cushion cover

For covering the piping filler cord, measure the amount of piping you think you will need and add about 10cm (4in) to allow for joins. The strips should be about 5cm (2in) wide so that when folded in half lengthways around the cord, the resulting fabric width is 2.5cm (1in).

Find the bias of the fabric by folding diagonally so that the selvedge is parallel with the adjacent edge. Mark strips of the required width parallel to the diagonal fold and cut out the strips. To make one long strip, pin the strips together, end to end with right sides facing, and stitch along the straight grain. Press seams open and trim the seam allowances flush with the strip edge.

Lay the cord along the centre on the wrong side of the strip, then fold the fabric around it so that the raw edges are brought together. Stitch by machine, close to the cord, using a special piping foot or a zipper foot. Trim the seam to 1.5cm (⅝in).

Cut out a front and a back cushion cover piece. Align the raw edges and pin and tack the piping to the right side of the cover front. Snip the piping seam allowance at the corners, leaving a 5cm (2in) overlap where the piping ends meet. Stitch around the cushion. To join the piping ends, pull back the fabric cover and trim both ends of piping filler cord so that they butt together. Trim the fabric so that one end turns under and overlaps the other to give a neat finished edge. Complete the stitching of the seam.

Leaving an opening for the zip and with right sides together, stitch the back of the cover to the front along the opening edge so that the piping is sandwiched between the layers. Press the seam open. Stitch the zip in place one side at a time. Complete the cover as for a cushion cover with a zip in the seam (see page 47).

Cord

Ready-made decorative cords come in all kinds of thicknesses and colours and can be made from cotton, wool, silk or a mixture of fibres. Some cords have gold or other metallic thread running through them that adds sparkle and a touch of luxury. It is also possible to find wonderful antique cords.

Cords designed for inserting as piping come with a flange attached which is usually a piece of cotton webbing. These can be used exactly as you would a length of covered piping. Cords without flanges have to be hand sewn after the cushion cover is made.

Attaching cord to a cushion cover

Leave a small opening in the seam when making the cover. Hand sew the cord over the seam line around the edge of a finished cushion cover. Insert each end into the opening in the seam and secure in place. Alternatively, wrap each end of the cord tightly with a matching thread and butt the ends together neatly where they join. Cord can be looped to make a bow at each cushion corner and stitched into place by oversewing.

Tassels and fringes

Fringes make interesting finishes for cushion covers and these are hand sewn to the completed cushion cover as for cords. Some fringes also come with a flange webbing and can be inserted in a seam line like piping. Tassels add an ornate touch to cushions and bolsters. They are available in a wide range of shapes, sizes and colours, but can also be made by hand.

Attaching a flanged fringe to a cushion cover

Stitch the fringe to the right side of the front of the cover along the seam line, with the fringed edge pointing towards the centre of the cover. Make the cover as for a cover with piping, sandwiching the fringe between the two sides of the cover.

Cord and braid

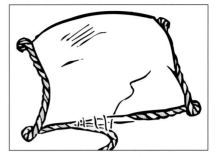

1 Hand sew cord over the seam line, forming loops at each corner if desired. Secure the ends inside the cover.

Fringes and tassels

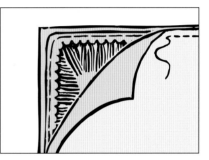

1 As for a piped cover, stitch the fringe to the right side of the front before joining on the back of the cover.

▲ The fluffy, colourful fringing perfectly complements the printed Manolo Blahnik shoe drawings on the cushions. This type of fringing has a flange and can be machine sewn between the two sides of fabric when the cushion is being assembled. Fringes can be specially dyed for individual projects.

Borders

Both flat borders and ruffles add an extra touch of luxury to what would otherwise be an unexceptional cushion or pillow. They are worth taking extra trouble over, as they help enhance the pillow or cushion fabric.

Flat borders

Flat borders around cushions or pillow cases stand out like a flap. The cushion or pillow is encased within a stitched line and made accessible by a zipped or buttoned opening. A single border can be made either from the same fabric as the rest of the cover or in a contrasting fabric. A double border is essentially two single borders, the under border being slightly larger than the top border.

Making a single border cover

Make a cushion cover as for a cover with a zip across the back (see page 47) but allowing extra fabric on all four sides for the border, as well as the usual seam allowance

all around the edge. A standard border or flap is 5cm (2in) deep. Once all the edges of the cover are stitched together, trim the seam allowances and clip the corners diagonally. Press the seam open and turn right side out. Press flat, keeping the seams exactly on the edge and making the corners sharp.

On the back of the cover (zipped side), tack the front and the back together along the border line and machine stitch. Alternatively, work satin stitch along the border line and then, if you want, work a second line of satin stitch outside the first. Then remove the tacking.

To make a cover with a contrasting single border, cut the cushion cover pieces to the size of a cover without a border and insert the zip in the centre of the back piece (see page 47). Then cut the borders.

Each side of the cushion requires two strips of fabric, the size of the finished width of a single border (plus two seam allowances), multiplied by the length of the cushion cover, plus two border widths.

Stitch together, the lengths of border to the cushion fabric, leaving the ends at each corner to trail. Join the border strips at the corner by mitring (see page 75) or butt the ends together, stitching straight across the adjacent border having previously trimmed the surplus and pressed the seam flat. By abutting the borders you should finish up with two parallel borders the length of the finished cushion, with the other two set between them. Once the borders are joined to the front and back of the cushion, complete the cover as for a single border.

Single border

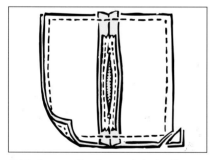

1 Make the cover with a zip across the back, adding extra all around for the border. Trim and press seam open.

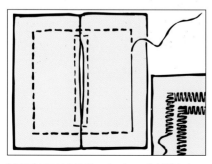

2 Turn the cover right side out and press flat. Stitch along the border line, using straight stitch or satin stitch.

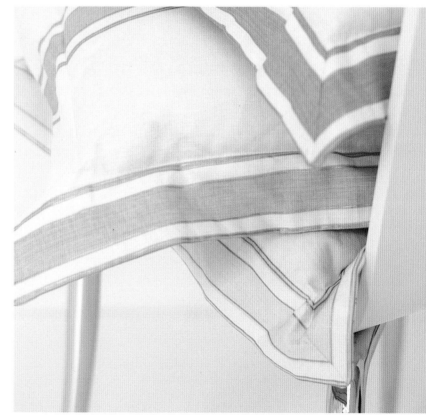

▲ These simple linen cushions use the stripe in the fabric as a border which is set outside the edge of the cushion pad. The stripe is cut and sewn to each side of the central panel before the cushion cover is made up. Each corner is mitred, with the stripe carefully matched for a neat, geometric finish.

Double border

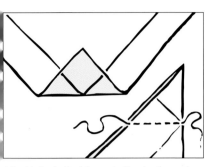 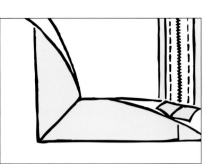 

1 Double the depth of the required border all around. Press the border to the wrong side and mitre the corners.

2 Trim the mitre seam allowances and press the seam open. Turn the corners right side out.

3 Determine the final depth of the border. Join the front of the cover to the back and stitch along the border lines.

Ruffles

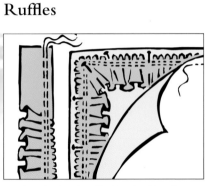

1 Make and gather the ruffle. Pin and tack it to the cushion cover front before stitching on the back.

◀ *Two contrasting finishing techniques combine to make a pleasing effect. The cord piping gives the chair a very linear appearance, enhanced by the use of striped fabric. Meanwhile, the floral-print cushion cover is finished off with a frivolous, deep-frilled edging.*

Making a double border cover

A cushion cover with a double border is made in the same way as a single border, but double the depth of the required finished border must be added on to the lengths, plus the seam allowances. Make up the back section as for a cover with a zip across the back (see page 47). Fold the borders to the wrong side and press. With right sides together, mitre each corner (see page 75). Trim the mitred corners, turn right side out and press. Lay the two sides together, wrong sides facing, and tack along the border line, catching the raw edge of the border inside the cover. Machine stitch closed.

Ruffles

Ruffles add a softening touch to cushions and other furnishings, and are generally made from light, filmy fabrics or country-cottage prints. But, with imagination and a bold choice of colour, ruffles need not be restricted to the boudoir; they can be used to make a strong impact anywhere.

Attaching a ruffle to a cover

Make a ruffle twice the circumference of the required finished cushion cover. The ruffle can either have a narrow hem or be doubled over so that the raw edges of both layers are aligned. Run a running stitch around the raw edges of the length of the ruffle. Pull the thread to gather the ruffle, then pin and tack it to the right side of the front piece of the cover, aligning the raw edges. Complete the cushion cover in the usual way, catching the ruffle seam allowance in between the front and back sections of the cover.

Covers for seating

The possibilities of covering furniture with fabric are as exciting as they are endless. Do you go for loosely draped, unstructured sheets of cloth that billow like dust covers over an old sofa? Or do you prefer smart, tailored little numbers with tucks and pleats and artfully placed buttons, which might disguise the awfulness of a battered dining chair?

The art of adding fabric to furniture opens up a wealth of decorative possibilities. Small seats can be tightly covered, whereas long, low benches look stunning when loosely dressed; deck-chair frames can be given a new lease of life covered in a different fabric, or natty little folding stools can be sharpened up with new, slung canvas.

Fine detailing adds sophistication to the disguise. Use eyelets, buttons, loops and ties, tassels and trims. Invent new ways of using old materials. However, don't lose sight of the practicalities and the function of the piece, even if your own ingenuity takes over.

Deck and director's chairs

Deck chairs are a simple combination of fabric and wood, a construction that folds neatly away. They have a timeless quality and a modest structure that have endured for many years. However, it is difficult to disassociate them from their exterior environments of beach, garden or on board a ship, although they can look wonderful in a large children's room or bathroom.

A director's chair has much the same feel as a deck chair, but because of its higher seat and more obvious 'chair-like' qualities, it is useful in informal settings in the home. For deck chairs, director's chairs and other folding chairs, the seat and back are made from pieces of fabric slung between two bars, and attaching it to the frame could not be simpler. The method for fitting new fabric depends on the design of the chair and whether the frame needs to be, or can be, taken apart. Where 'sleeves' of fabric can be made, these are ideal for sheathing the bars of the frame for seat and back, but where the design does not allow for this, fabric can be attached by stretching it around the bars on either side of the seat or back, and then stapling it to the outer edges with a heavy-duty staple gun. A

◀ *Traditional striped canvas can give a whole new lease of life to ancient deck-chair frames. In this instance, mixing the colours of two canvases, which have an identical design, creates a pleasing and visually interesting contrast while also retaining a sense of continuity.*

▲ *While pastel cottons and delicate chintzes make attractive upholstery fabrics, they are difficult to keep clean and are vulnerable to wear and tear. A sensible choice for hard-working kitchen or dining-room chairs is the tough and durable finish shown here, achieved by tightly binding thin rope over a wooden chair frame.*

sleeve comprises a loop of fabric, secured down the inner side of each frame bar with a line of machine stitching. If the chair design requires the sleeve to fit over a place where the frame is joined, holes can be punched in the fabric and large eyelet holes secured before reassembling. Choose strong fabrics that are not going to rot or tear. Try unusual material such as tapestry or wool tartan.

Folding stools

Small, low, X-frame stools, made from timber or metal, work well in interior set-tings. They make useful 'occasional' seating,

doubling up as small tables for lightweight items such as books or newspapers. A few of them, dotted around a room filled with other styles of furniture, help to punc-tuate space. For a more minimalist interior, try a row of them using brightly coloured fabrics against a plain white wall, or mix different patterns on the same theme: for example, children's prints of animals or cowboys to make a perfect ensemble for a young child's bedroom.

The methods for attaching the fabric, whether a sleeve is made or the fabric is stapled, are the same as those for deck chairs.

Drop-in seats

◀ *These blue-and-white checked dining-chair drop-in seats complement the nineteenth-century Swedish-style table and chairs. The seats provide bursts of colour to contrast with the many different wood textures found in this typically Scandinavian setting.*

The tricky art of fixed upholstery for sofas, chairs and day-beds is often best left to a professional, for when done properly it is worth the investment. However, to re-cover the upholstered seat of a drop-in dining chair is relatively straightforward.

A chair with a drop-in seat is usually a dining chair, and the seat lifts right out. It consists of a simple wooden frame covered in padding (horsehair and wadding) which rests on and is supported by strips of webbing pulled taut across the frame. A calico covering is stretched tightly over the padding and fixed to the underside of the frame by tacks. The top fabric is applied over the calico and fixed in the same way. The underside is finished off with a piece of hessian with its edges turned under for neatness. If the webbing is still good, and the padding is in reasonable condition – it may need some building up – you should not need to strip everything off.

Re-covering a drop-in seat

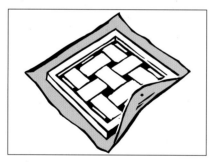

1 *Bring the sides of the new calico to the underside of the frame. Secure with a tack at the centre of each side.*

2 *Smoothing the calico as you proceed, continue to add tacks along each side of the frame.*

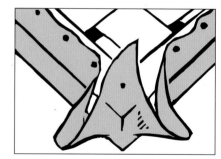

3 *Pull the calico taut over the corners and tack. Fold a pleat to each side of the tack and secure.*

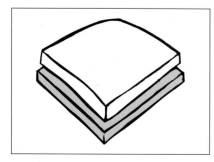

4 *Turn the seat over. Lay in place a new piece of wadding the same size as the top of the seat.*

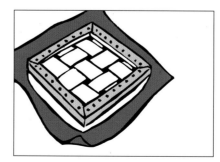

5 *Keeping the wadding in place, lay the seat upside-down on the new outer covering, centring it carefully.*

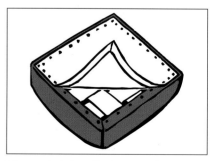

6 *Cut out a fresh piece of hessian. Turn under the hem and tack the hessian to the underside of the frame.*

For the fabric covering of a drop-in seat, customized fabric is always more challenging than simply using fabric as it comes. Two strongly contrasting colours could be stitched together and the joined fabric could be positioned over the seat so that the seam runs centrally across the chair – front to back or side to side. A pair of chairs with a weathered patina (see pages 14–15) would be a stunning focal point with covered seats in burgundy and indigo silk.

Re-covering a drop-in seat

The only tools you will need are a pair of scissors, a tape measure, a hammer, a mallet and a chisel. The materials needed to cover the padded seat are a sheet of wadding big enough to cover the top of the seat, a piece of calico to fit over the seat, a piece of upholstery fabric for the outer covering of the seat (big enough to go over the top of the seat and the underside of the frame), 1cm (⅜in) fine tacks and black upholstery linen or hessian for finishing the underside of the seat.

With the seat upside-down and using the mallet and chisel, remove the tacks securing the old hessian. In the same way remove the tacks that hold the old outer fabric covering in place. Open out the hessian and the old fabric and use them to make paper patterns for the new pieces, making sure that the pattern allows for an extra 5cm (2in) all around for either turning under or stretching over the underside of the frame.

Remove the old top layer of wadding and discard. Beneath this should be a layer of calico, under which is the horsehair. If necessary, remove the old calico, but if it is sufficiently intact, keep it in place. Cut a new piece of calico using the paper pattern made from the old outer cover. Lay the seat upside-down on the calico and bring the sides up and over the edge of the frame. Using the hammer, secure the calico with a tack at the centre of each side. Smoothing the calico as you go, add tacks along each side of the frame. Pull the calico taut over the corners and tack. Fold a pleat to each side of the tack and trim away the excess fabric. Turn the seat over. Cut a new piece of wadding to exactly the same size as the top of the seat. This is a soft layer that prevents the spiky horsehair from coming through the fabric. Lay the wadding on top of the seat.

Using the paper pattern made from the old outer fabric, cut out a piece of fabric large enough to go over the seat to the underside of the frame. Lay the seat (with the wadding on top) upside-down on the new outer covering. Tack the fabric to the frame.

Using the paper pattern made from the old hessian, cut out a fresh piece of hessian. Turn under the hem and fasten the hessian to the underside of the frame, tacking at 2.5cm (1in) intervals.

Woven webbing

For a natural, textured look try using upholsterer's webbing tape about 5cm (2in) wide, woven across the frame of a stool or perhaps on a simple dining chair where the seat has gone, leaving an empty frame. A very stylish effect can be achieved by this relatively simple method. You will need enough webbing to be divided equally into short strips that will be fixed side by side across the frame to create the 'warp' and the same quantity to use as the 'weft', the layer that weaves in and out of the fixed layer. The length of each strip (warp or weft) will be the distance across the top of the frame from edge to edge, plus an amount that can wrap around to the underside of the frame for securing (with tacks or a staple gun) out of sight. If you want the fixing to be a feature, and therefore to be seen, you could use various types of upholsterer's decorative studs.

Cut and fasten the first layer of webbing, making sure each piece is pulled very taut before fixing. The seat will be bound to sag a little as body weight is put on it, so bear this in mind and perhaps allow some excess that can be unrolled for retightening. Weave the second layer of strips between the first, again fixing each end in the same way.

Webbing tape, commonly made of jute, can be dyed so that a colourful, contrasting chequerboard effect can be achieved with relative ease. Alternatively, it is possible to buy coloured webbing of the sort that edges carpets or rugs.

◄ *Webbing can make for an extremely comfortable chair. It is very versatile, can be easily replaced and comes in different colours to match any decor. Neutral webbing can be dyed in vibrant, colourful shades and two or more colours can be interwoven to achieve interesting designs.*

Loose covers

▶ *Like 1950s summer dresses out to tea, these linen chair covers in ice-cream shades look spruce and elegant. Their sharp colours are perfectly contrasted against the bleached wood floor and the simple white tablecloth. A row of self-covered buttons is a witty addition.*

As their name implies, loose covers are not fixed to the furniture they cover. They might have ties or zips, or even button fastenings, but their essential character is removability. First, there is a practical element governing the choice of fabric for such a cover. Second, the fabric can be used to glorious decorative effect with stitching, folding, pleats, knots – or by simply throwing it over.

Designs for loose covers
The shape of the furniture dictates the look of the loose cover, whether it has a tailored look, where the cover starts to resemble formal upholstery, or a more casual, unstructured effect. The furniture is the mannequin, around which the fabric is pinned, tucked, pleated and stitched, and through experiment the cover will take shape.

Squarish arms on a sofa, for example, can be made more attractive by adding an unexpected kick pleat here and there, and by double pleating the fabric a really textured look can be achieved. Try using a contrasting fabric inside a pleat for further emphasis.

Detail is the all-important thing. Take a leaf from fashion *haute couture* and add exquisite touches that will transform a plain cover, such as punched eyelets along the base of a skirt, or rows of hand-sewn buttons in glorious glassy colours. Fringing and tassels add texture and give a more luxurious feel. To the front of a pleat add a tab of fabric or tape and a bright bold button to fasten. Along the base attach a band of Petersham ribbon to a plain fabric for definition and added colour, or hand stitch in thick tapestry wool bold crisscrosses or dots. A row of small pearly buttons down the back of a white linen cover – quite a tailored affair over an upright dining chair – would look very impressive.

Most loose covers have a skirt of some sort which runs around the base and is a separately made piece that extends to the floor. Use double, overlapping layers in the same cloth or one that has a distinctly different texture. Fold wide box pleats around the front edge of a long sofa, and for the two shorter sides, run tiny little pleats or use two-coloured fabrics for a striped effect.

The beauty of making loose, as opposed to fixed, covers is that it allows you to play around with the shape a little more. Take the skirt from the seat height or make a pleat in

Making a loose cover for a dining chair

1 Pin the two back pieces of fabric together wrong side out. Remove from the chair, tack and stitch.

2 Cut out the valance piece and a piece the same size for the lining. Stitch together with right sides facing.

3 Turn the valance right side out and pin it to the chair seat piece with right sides facing. Stitch.

the centre at the back. By taking this idea further you can disguise the shape of a sofa or chair quite considerably.

Making a loose cover for a chair

Measure the front of the chair back from the top of the chair to the seat and then across the width of the back, allowing for the thickness of the frame. Cut out a piece of fabric to these dimensions, plus a 5cm (2in) seam allowance all around. Measure the back of the chair from the top to the floor, then measure the back of the chair across the widest part (usually at the base of the chair), again allowing for the thickness of the frame. Cut out a piece of fabric to these dimensions, plus a 3cm (1¼in) seam allowance.

With the wrong sides facing, pin these two fabric pieces together over the back of the chair, making sure that the cover will slip off easily and keeping the proposed seam lines symmetrical. Remove the cover, tack along the proposed seam line and remove the pins. With the cover still the wrong side out, try it on the chair again and adjust, if necessary, making sure that the tacking stops precisely at the level of the chair seat. Remove, and machine stitch. Trim the seam allowances. Set this piece aside.

Measure from the seat of the chair to the floor and then around the legs of the chair at the base, from one back leg around the front legs and the other back leg. Cut out a piece of fabric to these dimensions, allowing for a 7.5cm (3in) overlap at each side of

the back and adding a 1.5cm (⅝in) seam allowance all around. Cut a lining piece exactly the same size from the same fabric. With right sides together and raw edges aligned, stitch these two pieces together, leaving the edge that will fit around the chair seat opening. Trim the seam allowances and then clip the two corners diagonally. Press the seam open. Turn right sides out and press flat with the seam aligned along the edge. Tack the raw edges together. Set this valance piece aside.

Cut a piece of fabric to fit the chair seat exactly, with a 1.5cm (⅝in) seam allowance all around. Lay this piece wrong side uppermost on the chair seat, then pin the valance to the chair seat with right sides together and raw edges aligned, leaving the extended bit at the back free. Take the pinned pieces off the chair, tack and remove the pins. Stitch and then slip the back section of the cover back onto the chair (still wrong side out). Pin it to the chair seat section where the two sections meet at the back of the seat. Remove, tack and stitch.

Trim the seam allowances around the chair seat. Then cut the two front corners of the chair seat section diagonally and notch the corresponding corners on the valance section. Press the seam open and then press it towards the centre of the seat.

Cut four lengths of ribbon or make four fabric ties (see page 77). Then cut a piece of fabric to line the back valance drop, including a 1.5cm (⅝in) seam allowance all

around. Put the cover on the chair wrong side out and pin the lining to the back valance drop, with right sides together. Remove and then position the ties along the seam. Tack and stitch, catching the ends of the ties in the seam. Trim the seam allowances and corners and press the seam open.

Remove all the tacking. Turn the whole cover right side out and press. If desired, line the underside of the seat area to enclose the raw edges, slip stitching the lining in place.

Put the cover on the chair right side out. Hand sew ties to the front valance to correspond to the ties at the back.

Covering furniture with throws

Just throwing over a length of fabric and allowing it to fall naturally into folds or gathers is perhaps the simplest way of covering furniture. Blankets, shawls or quilts can be mixed against each other and displayed against a backdrop of bleached white cotton first draped over the furniture. Large pieces of cloth can be 'handkerchief-knotted' on their corners or around the legs of a chair.

To make a very simple throw, sew together two pieces of fabric, as though you were making a cushion, add a layer of wadding or interlining between them and when turned right side out, secure the opening by hand. You will have a lightly padded square or rectangle. Stitch flat buttons or small loops of cord across the surface for decoration and hang the whole thing over the back or arm of a sofa or day-bed.

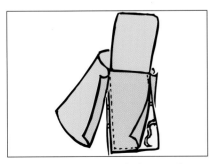

4 *Pin the chair seat section to the back cover section along the back of the chair seat and stitch.*

5 *With the cover wrong side out on the chair, pin a lining to the back valance. Stitch, catching in the ties.*

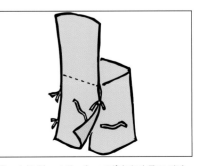

6 *Turn right side out. Line the seat if desired. Then stitch ties to the front valance section to match the back ties.*

Bedding

From theatrical fantasy to pared-down practicality,
the decoration and covering of your bed will undoubtedly
reflect your personal style. The bedroom is an
intimate environment, whether or not it is shared with
another person. For some, the bedroom is simply
a sleeping space, while for others it may also be an office –
where telephone and other communications to the
outside world must be on hand – or indeed a play area,
with shelving and boxes for toys and children's books.

As well as considering the needs of the bedroom, the requirements of the bed itself may be wildly different – having to double up as a sofa during the day, or perhaps exist as an area of private space as a 'room within a room', curtained and canopied.

Perhaps the most exciting challenge in decorating a bed is that it is three-dimensional. There are both horizontal and vertical planes to consider. This offers considerable scope for the imagination. Whether it is a simple divan, a painted metal bunk or ornately carved wooden four-poster, a bed provides surfaces and shapes to decorate, cover or completely conceal. The whole of the bed, and its immediate surroundings, can become an exciting mix of tactile materials, whether fabric, mosaic, paint or even paper.

Bed-linen

When considering the basic bed-linen, you might choose to look for old, good-quality linen sheets in specialist shops or markets, or decorate newer cotton sheets with a simple stitched motif or a row of buttons. Along the edges of plain sheets or duvet covers, the addition of a striped piping or a border of appliquéd shapes can transform and give character to a neutral surface. Imagine a row of coloured cut-out zoo animals or letters of the alphabet in line across the end of a child's duvet cover.

While basic sheeting may be unpatterned and – typically – white, covers, quilts or valances present a good opportunity to introduce colour and pattern. Imagine striped-cotton quilt covers over white cotton sheets, or linen in faded gentle colours mixed with antique patchwork quilts – or perhaps with a bold contemporary duvet design (provided a colour link is established).

Whether for a tiny baby's cradle or a massive *lit bateau*, warmth should be an immediate consideration. For cold nights, consider chunky warm blankets in bold checks, either as additional throws or in the place of quilts or duvets.

Bed valances – or wonderfully named 'dust ruffles' – can conceal unattractive bed bases or provide curtaining for under-the-

◀ *Striped and checked fabrics have been mixed and matched in this bedroom, but limiting the colour scheme to blue and white means that the finished look is crisp and clean rather than jumbled. By day the canopies strung across the beds provide shade from the sunlight; by night they create a cosy cocoon.*

▲ *On entering this bedroom, the eye is drawn to the unusual wrought-iron headboard. Its exaggerated Gothic styling, resembling ornamental railing, is made all the more striking by its juxtaposition with warm colours and soft, highly textured fabrics: the sunny yellow walls and cosy-looking bedspread with its vivid relief design of sunbursts.*

bed storage. These are made to fit individual beds, usually with pleats at each corner, and could be made in the same fabric as the main bed cover or in a contrasting material. For added detail, include a border along the base of the skirt in a different fabric or braid. Alternatively, you could box pleat the whole skirt.

Decorating surroundings

As well as layering fabrics on the bed itself, a partial or complete framework of fabric 'walls' can be created over and around the bed from gathered or stretched material. A contemporary metal version of the ornate four-poster provides a structure from which to hang fabrics, simply tied or tabbed at

the top. Lightweight muslin can fall airily to the floor; double-layered or heavier cloth can provide warmth and texture. Chunky metal eyelets, punched through the fabric, can be slotted onto a pole, while simple canopies can be supported by a bracket or short pole projecting from the wall above the bed.

Headboards provide support, and can also feature as key elements to cover and decorate. Here, a stamped metal headboard, for example, can provide a contrasting backdrop for pillows in, say, a crisp white-and-grey stripe. Hang quilted fabrics over a fixed head end; mix stripes and floral patterns, canvas and delicate embroidery, or richly textured tapestries and white piqué to create the style you want.

Pillow cases, valances and throws

The vast range of bedding and bed-linen now available makes the bed the key element in the bedroom's design. How the bed is 'dressed' makes the ultimate design statement.

Pillow cases

Bed pillows should be comfortable and not so numerous that you need to discard most of them in order to sleep! Rectangular or square, on their own or with a long bolster beneath, they are often the focus of the bed.

Their cases are essentially fabric bags like small duvet covers and their construction is much the same. At their most plain they are a top and a base stitched together with a pocket to keep the pillow held inside. They can also have a border all around as on an 'Oxford' pillow case.

Add a line of buttoning, embroidery, lace or a fabric border and a pillow case is instantly transformed. A blanket stitch along the open edge can be a simple detail. For a tailored look, use cases that have a flap around the edge, which can be made from the same fabric as the rest of the case or in a contrast. Layering plain on stripe on check, linking the colour, can be smart and can incorporate a combination of fabrics used elsewhere on other parts of the bed. For an instant monogram try hand stencilling bold letters or motifs, using a permanent dye. These are much cheaper than the embroidered ones that have now become collector's items, although these, if you can find them still in good condition, are very beautiful.

▲ *The key to bed-linen is to keep it simple – but that does not mean it always has to be white. Here, although white is the basic colour, the crisp blue-and-green ginghams dominate and there are similar colours in the bed cover to provide a harmonious link. The bedstead, with its simple curved iron frame, accentuates the cool, clean overall effect.*

Making a pillow case

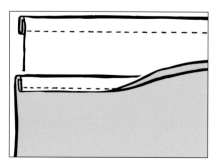

1 Cut out a single piece of fabric for the case and stitch a double hem along each short edge.

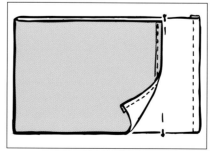

2 Fold the fabric so the right sides are together and the flap extends 15cm (6in) past the end. Pin into position.

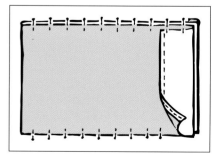

3 Turn the case over and fold the flap back so the folded edge aligns with the hemmed edge. Pin into position.

Old cottons and linens, once thoroughly washed, make beautiful pillow cases. Smart checks and stripes in cool colours can be added as borders, flaps or edgings.

Making a pillow case

Pillow cases should be made from cotton or poplin, or linen. For a pillow with a pocket to hold in the pillow, cut a single piece of fabric twice the length of the pillow plus a total of 20cm (8in) for the inside flap and for the double hem allowances, by the width of the pillow case, plus an extra 3cm (1¼in) for seam allowances.

Along each short side, turn under and stitch a 1cm double (⅜in) hem (see page 75). Fold the fabric right sides together, the length of the pillow from one end, so that the flap extends 15cm (6in) past the doubled-over pillow case. Pin the raw edges together. Then turn the case over and fold the flap back on the case so that the folded edge aligns with the hemmed edge. Pin the raw edges of the flap to the other layers and tack. Remove the pins and machine stitch through all the layers 1.5cm (⅝in) from the edges. Pink the raw edges or zigzag stitch them and trim. Turn right side out. The flap will now be on the inside of the finished pillow case.

Bed valances (dust ruffles)

These bed dressings form a skirt between the base of the mattress and the floor. The skirt is typically attached to a flat piece of fabric

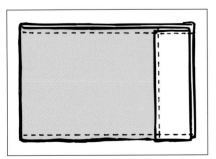

4 Tack and machine stitch through all the layers. Pink the raw edges or zigzag stitch them and turn right side out.

that sits between the mattress and the bed base. Because it is hidden, this can be made of inexpensive lining. The skirt, in a more interesting fabric, can be flat, with tailored kick pleats at each corner, or, as on beds with a fixed head and foot end, the corner pleats can be split to fall either side of the bed leg.

Box pleats, although taking a considerable amount of fabric – three times that for a flat skirt – are smart and straightforward and, using a contrasting fabric in the pleats, can give a striking effect. For a more sculptural finish, instead of pleats at the corners, simply join the fabric using punched eyelets and tied cord. For a softer effect, gather the skirt into rich folds of crumpled linen, muslin or shot taffeta silk. Whichever style you choose to make, careful measuring and estimating of the amount of fabric required are essential as a valance will not work if there is not enough material in it. As valances tend not be washed as often as covers and pillow cases, a more robust fabric can be used.

Throws

A throw suggests casualness and spontaneity. It is intended to go over all other bedding and provides an extra layer for additional warmth, perhaps used only occasionally and otherwise stored at the end of the bed. Throws can also be a useful device for concealing a mixture of bedding beneath and thus 'tidying' a bed that perhaps by day becomes a sofa.

Throws are generally made from a rectangle of fabric, cut large enough to cover the bed end to end and to fall to the floor on both sides. They are then hemmed and possibly lined as well. Throws can be used with valances, in which case the fabric is cut to fall only part of the way down each side of the bed in order to reveal the valance beneath. Throws may be plain or quilted, with additional borders or edgings that add colour or texture. As the throw is intended to be folded down once the bed is in use, a heavier fabric can be used.

◀ *Cool blue and cream combine to be the dominant theme here. The wonderful midnight-blue backdrop behind the ice-cream swirls of the bed frame is picked up in the checks and stripes and* toile de Jouy *patterns of the various items of bed-linen. The top quilt is reversible, using the three different fabrics to great effect.*

Duvet covers

Making a simple duvet cover

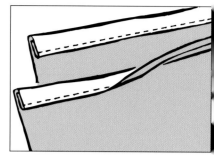

1 Cut two pieces for the cover. Along the opening edge of each piece, stitch a 3cm (1¼in) double hem.

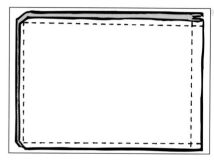

2 Stitch the two pieces together with wrong sides facing, leaving the hemmed edges open. Trim.

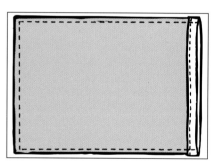

3 Press the seam open, then turn the cover wrong side out and press flat. Stitch again and turn right side out.

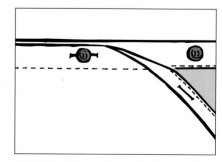

4 Make buttonholes along the opening edge about 25cm (10in) apart and sew on the buttons to match.

▲ *This is an inspired use of an awkward space – the bed does not attempt to look small. Understated cream and white cotton bed-linen, plus a minimal use of black-and-white traditional mattress ticking, create an elegant interior. Subtly stitched motifs criss-cross the duvet cover and a simple line of stitching runs around the edge.*

Duvets have largely replaced sheets and blankets, and their covers are easy both to use and to clean. Essentially two pieces of rectangular fabric joined on three sides, they are a bag for the duvet to fit inside. A large pocket can be made at the open end, to prevent the duvet from slipping out – just like the pocket on a traditional pillow case.

Alternatively, the duvet cover opening can be fastened with ties or buttons. Both these devices can be used to bring contrast and colour, such as checked red-and-white ties on a plain cover or bold tartan ribbons to fasten one in striped ticking. Buttons can be bold and eye-catching, while the buttonholes can be made using brightly coloured thread. If you prefer to keep things simple, just use press studs or a zip fastening.

For a more subtle approach, add piping along the seam between the two layers of fabric. On a bed that is covered entirely in white, a piped line of blue-and-white gingham or multicoloured floral pattern adds just a hint of detail and colour, perhaps picking up another fabric in the room.

For children's bedding, a duvet cover with one fabric on the top and another beneath is fun and can transform a space simply by being reversed. Another way of adding interest is to mimic a patchwork quilt and use large squares to create a chequerboard pattern of two or three bold colours, or a combination of different sizes of stripes.

Cotton is really the only fabric to consider for duvet covers as it is easy to wash and is comfortable to touch. It should not be too heavy. For a double duvet cover, you may not be able to find wide enough fabric, so you will have to join pieces together before cutting out your first pieces to size. Always join with a full width of fabric in the centre, giving you two seam lines.

To make the joins more interesting, add a strip of fabric between the two pieces you are joining together on either side. Press seams towards the insets and then make up as described above.

Making a simple duvet cover

Cut two pieces of fabric, each a little longer than the duvet itself, plus a total of 10cm (4in) for hems and seam allowance, by the width of the duvet, plus 7.5cm (3in) for the seam allowances. Along the opening edge of each piece, machine stitch a double 3cm (1¼in) hem (see page 75).

To join the two pieces together, first pin them together with wrong sides facing and raw edges aligned, leaving the hemmed edges open. Stitch 2cm (¾in) from the edge. Trim the seam allowances to 1.5cm (⅝in) and then clip off the two seam allowance corners diagonally. Press the seam open

Making the buttonholes

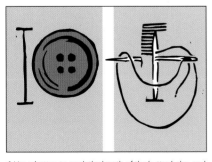

1 Use a button to mark the length of the buttonholes, and buttonhole stitch around the slit, oversewing at each end.

and turn the cover wrong side out so that the right sides are together. Press the seam flat, aligning the seam line along the fold. Stitch 2cm (¾in) from the edge. Turn right side out and press.

Making the buttonholes on the cover

Mark the positions for the buttonholes along one edge of the opening about 25cm (10in) apart. Use a button to mark the length of the buttonholes, allowing for the button thickness. If you are making the buttonholes by machine, follow the instructions in your sewing machine manual.

If you are sewing the buttonholes by hand, use a pair of small scissors to cut the buttonhole. Start by oversewing the cut at one end several times. Buttonhole stitch down one side of the slit, oversew the other end, turn

the fabric around and buttonhole stitch up the other side. Fasten the thread end into the end of the buttonhole on the wrong side. Sew on the buttons to correspond with the positions of the buttonholes.

Making tie fastenings for the cover

The simple duvet cover can be fastened with ties instead of buttonholes. Use lengths of ribbon with the raw edge slip stitched over, and secure them to each side of the duvet opening in pairs.

Alternatively, ties can be made from strips of fabric, either the same as the cover or in a contrasting pattern. Cut strips about 30cm (12in) long by 6cm (2½in) wide, fold over and press a 1cm (½in) hem on all sides. Fold the strips in half so that the long sides meet, wrong sides together. Top stitch all around and stitch in place as for ribbons.

◀ *A blue-and-white checked gingham duvet cover and buttoned pillows lie comfortably crumpled against the white linen sheet on this simple bed. The interior is cool and understated, with neutral background colours that allow the bed covers to dominate. The gingham is echoed in the frame on the cupboard and helps to unite the theme.*

Bed hangings

▲ *An all-white decorative scheme is often the most striking. Here the choice of bed drapery was influenced by the distressed plaster walls and wooden shutters; the pillows and bedspread, with their unusual leaf-shaped edging, and the swathes of white fabric suspended from a half-corona would not look out of place in a medieval bedchamber.*

Extending the decoration of a bed up into its surrounding space, by hanging fabrics around it or over it, can transform a straightforward bed into something extraordinary and magical.

Imagine climbing into a sleeping bunk on a train and closing the curtains to create your own private space, or lying beneath tented canvas, peering out at the stars. These two effects can be easily recreated in your bedroom with a little forethought and planning.

Curtains can become walls, to surround a bed completely, either hung from a frame such as a traditional four-poster, or as a screen, between ceiling and floor. This is effective, for example, in a wide alcove, where a bed might be positioned sideways to the wall.

Fabric hangings to divide or create a space may either hang like curtains, whether from poles or from a support such as a timber canopy or 'pelmet', or be stretched like a screen between a support frame or fixed hooks.

Curtain-style bed hangings

When hung as curtains, if the heading is on show – usually where a tubular frame is fitted above a bed – simple headings such as eyelets, buttons, ties or tabs are most effective.

Tabs made from bands of fabric (see page 77) loop around the pole support. Consider making these in a fabric that contrasts in colour or pattern with the curtains themselves.

For a dramatic effect, use alternate coloured bands of fabric, such as pink and orange velvet atop a teal-coloured velvet curtain. Add brass buttons to the tabs, and to hold the curtains open, heavy rope tie-bands, and you have a wonderfully rich and dramatic bed arrangement.

Eyelets punched through the top of the curtains also provide a stylish method of hanging fabric around a bed, hanging the fabric either on a pole or on hooks from a low ceiling.

The beauty of bed hangings is that they have an inside and an outside, making an ideal opportunity to use two layers of completely contrasting fabrics. Imagine a crisp white linen on the inside and a heavy brocade on the outside, or a wide striped cotton lining a *toile de Jouy*. Obviously, the fullness of the fabric would depend on the effect required, and the type of fabric you were using.

Swathes of gathered fabric can be hung from traditional wooden pelmets as part of a four-poster, half-tester or corona. Usually these headings, which are not really seen except from inside the bed, are gathered with tape, like curtain headings.

Screen-style bed hangings

A flatter, screen-like effect can be achieved by sewing a sleeve at the top and base of a piece of fabric – a strong canvas works well, for instance – and by stretching it between a tubular frame. A side and an end, with a bed positioned sideways on to the wall, create a simple enclosure for a child's bunk bed, for example. Sew pockets onto the side of the fabric that faces the bed, for pyjamas or teddy bears.

The premise of using stretched fabric can be further extended to make a complete pitched roof for a bed. Try using sewn sleeves to slot over three horizontal poles, two parallel either side of the bed, and one higher up, centred over the middle section of the bed.

A flap, hanging part way down each side, can cleverly mimic a tent. For added detail, shape the edges or hang small key tassels. Similarly, a pole hanging above and across each end of the bed can support a length of fabric which, at the head end, can fall behind the pillows, thus creating a backdrop.

If you also cut the fabric long at the foot end, and attach strips of fabric or ribbon to either side, it will allow the fabric to be rolled up and tied to the poles like a rolled-up tent flap.

▶ *This sleeping area, little more than an alcove, could have had a rather claustrophobic atmosphere. Instead, a suspended canopy draws the eye up and across the ceiling, exaggerating the tiny space. A candle sconce and painted wall design provide interesting Gothic detail.*

Screens

Free-standing screens were once the interior item no discerning household was without, mainly because they acted as excellent draught excluders, protecting seating areas from the vastness of the room beyond. They have been much neglected of late, which is difficult to understand as they can be very decorative and act as clever room dividers. They are, in essence, a transportable wall.

Usually made in three or more hinged sections, which allow them to stand freely, screens can be constructed using timber or metal frames covered with canvas or fabric.

Free-standing screens make useful window coverings where a more familiar curtain or blind is perhaps difficult to install. And, in a low-ceilinged room where floor-to-ceiling windows have been designed to frame a view

beyond and a permanent covering would be a hindrance, screens come into their own, folding away when not required. If a screen is to move from place to place make sure that it is not too heavy.

Decorating a screen

Each side of a screen is on show to different sections of a room, so they can be decorated to display a different design style. The frames are more than just supports and form an integral part of the overall design. Timber frames can be stained, painted or polished, shaped across the top like a wooden pelmet or straight. You could commission a wrought-iron frame with splendid curved legs to support the fabric screen off the floor, and with decorative flourishes atop the

uprights. Artist's canvas stretched over a simple wooden frame can be painted directly with abstract or figurative designs.

All kinds of fabric can be used when making a screen; it all depends what kind of style you wish to create and the decorative or functional use the screen may have. Consider a sheer fabric that diffuses light, such as gauze or muslin, or perhaps a rough-textured linen or hessian. Fabric can be quilted or appliquéd or you could combine different fabrics (see pages 32–33).

To explore further the idea of a screen that allows light to penetrate, consider stretching chicken wire across a rough timber screen. Other metal sheeting can be substituted, from punched brass to galvanized steel. A solid wood screen covered in felt, with ribbons criss-crossing over it and secured with drawing pins, provides the perfect means for displaying cards, notes and other small pictures. Adapted for a children's room (remove the pins and use stitching instead) it can double up as a room divider and display board. Brown parcel paper is surprisingly elegant, and finished off with wonderful dome-headed pins around the edges of the frame makes a handsome screen, sufficiently neutral for all kinds of interiors.

Decoupage (see pages 20–21) can be exploited to wonderful effect on a flat screen. To use pasted paper to decorate a screen, a solid panel has to be attached to the frame. Use a thin plywood to keep the weight low if the entire panel is to be covered with paper. Alternatively, if the background to the cut-outs is to be painted, use stretched artist's canvas, primed and painted first.

Making a fabric-covered panel screen

Panel screens are made in sections from wood. The panels, once finished, are hinged together, so that each section can be at an angle to the next, thus allowing the whole screen to stand unaided.

Determine the height of the screen required and the width of each panel. As a guide, allow 180–200cm (72–78in) high by 50–60cm (20–24in) wide. You will need lengths of 5 x 2.5cm (2 x 1in) timber, wood

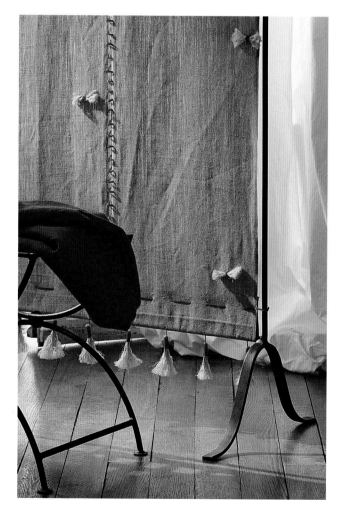

▶ *Two narrow strips of rough linen are suspended from a metal frame to form a screen, and divided by hand-stitched red cord. The cord is matched with little tassels made from twine. Linen, cord and tassels make a clever but simple combination, offset by the sturdy bleack metal frame.*

Making a fabric-covered panel screen

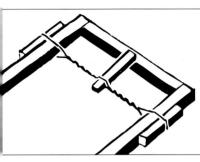

1 Secure the frame in place while the glue dries, using string and tourniquets to tighten the string.

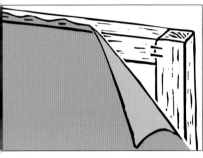

2 Keeping the fabric taut, staple one of the fabric pieces over the frame along the narrow outer edge of the frame.

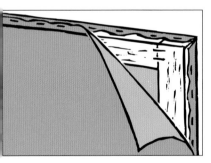

3 Attach the other fabric piece in the same way, stapling it in place along the narrow frame edge over the first piece.

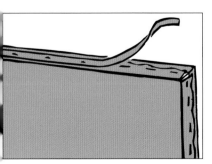

4 Tack the braid around the outer edge with upholstery nails or decorative studs. Hinge the panels together.

◀ Screens make useful backdrops and add colour and texture to areas with few features, as shown here. This simple screen is constructed from five hinged panels. A subtle cream-on-cream colourwash has been applied to the natural wooden frame, giving a beautiful hand-painted, textured finish that mimics the natural roughness of the stool.

glue, a staple gun, a metal square (for ensuring that the corners are true right angles), long woodworking clamps, and three hinges between each panel plus the fixing screws.

For each panel, cut two lengths of timber to the height of the screen, and two short pieces which will fit between the long ones. Make a rectangular frame, using wood glue to join each piece and staples to secure each join on both sides of the frame. Use the metal square to ensure that the corners are absolutely true, and clamp the frame in place while the glue dries, or alternatively tie it together with string using bits of wood as tourniquets to tighten.

Sometimes it may be necessary to have a cross-piece of timber positioned halfway down each panel to brace the frame and prevent it 'twisting'.

To cover the screen you will need fabric, interlining (if required), a staple gun or studs or upholstery tacks, and ribbon or braid for covering the joins, if desired. Cut the fabric pieces, sufficient to cover each panel plus allowances in the width and length to go around the side of the timber. When using braid or ribbon to finish off, leave the edges of the fabric raw. (If studs or upholstery nails are to be used, secure a folded fabric edge.) Keeping the fabric taut and straight, staple (or tack) one of the fabric pieces over the frame. The staples go into the outer narrow edge of the frame. When one piece is secured, attach the other piece. Tack the braid or ribbon in place with upholstery nails or studs.

When each panel is finished, screw hinges between each of the panels at the same height across the screen.

Table settings

How you choose to decorate a table will depend on a
number of factors: the table's style, its shape, the material
from which it is made, its setting and its particular role.
Tables may, for example, be covered by day to protect
their surfaces and only uncovered in the evening for
meals. Conversely, a large wooden refectory table in
a kitchen is highly functional, serving as both a dining
table and a work surface, so covering it with a cloth
would be impractical.

◄ *An attractive striped tablecloth in a heavy woven fabric is contrasted with the whisper-thin table napkins, which have matching brown tassels.*

▲ *A massive, unjoined long table such as the one above shouldn't be hidden underneath a tablecloth. Instead, the points of colour are provided by the ceramic plates.*

Tables that are not particularly attractive to look at, such as functional trestles or basic chipboard models, may require a permanent disguise, such as a casually draped cream dust sheet or a pair of old velvet curtains, while a beautiful table that is reserved for special dinner parties might be used at other times as a display area for decorative objects such as pots or vases of flowers, arrangements of shells and driftwood, or ornaments and curios.

Tablecloths

Tablecloths can be used purely for decoration or they can have a practical role – protecting a polished top, for instance, or covering up a less-than-attractive surface. They are easy to make. For the simplest of cloths, take a square of fabric – perhaps with country-style checks or deck-chair stripes – and simply machine sew a hem around the edges. Jazz up a plain cloth by sewing on a central panel of fabric, adding a wide border and mitring the corners. Punched eyelets in the corners of a cloth add detail and have an added bonus in that they can be anchored to the ground with pegs if you want to use the cloth for alfresco meals or picnics.

Although there is probably nothing to beat a fine white linen tablecloth for formal settings, a less expensive version in white mattress ticking with a fine herringbone weave can be just as effective – especially if it is starched. A rough-textured linen cloth in beige or taupe is equally attractive and creates a good neutral backdrop for colourful table settings. Many fabrics can be painted with relative ease. Stick to simple stencilled shapes, applied sparingly across the cloth, such as large, bold letters or images in keeping with a particular theme, be it Hallowe'en, Easter or Christmas. Keep the design uncomplicated and don't use too many colours or the finished result will look muddled and messy.

A combination of cloths in different sizes, placed one over the other, is both attractive and practical. Choose fabrics in contrasting textures (white linen over grey wool suiting or tweed) or contrasting colours (shiny silks in deep orange and purple). On a round table a square cloth draped over a circular one provides more visual interest than a single, large area of fabric. Always let the fabric trail on the ground a little. Heavier fabrics, such as chenille (a traditional covering for protecting polished dining tables when they are not in use) in a dark, rich crimson or moss green, can be trimmed with a rope fringe or edged with shimmering taffeta for elegant, candlelit settings. For long, oblong tables, a fitted cloth with pleated corners that falls to the floor (see pages 71–73) is particularly effective.

A temporary cover, such as a sheet of thick plywood, can help enlarge and make a table more sturdy. A plywood sheet can also be placed over a run of small trestles to make a large enough table for a dinner party.

Every sit-down meal requires a table setting. Even the most informal, impromptu snack calls for plates, cutlery and glasses, arranged in some kind of order. For sophisticated dinner parties, Sunday brunches or children's tea parties, the table can be set and decorated to create a particular atmosphere or theme. Start with a colour scheme before adding decorative details in the form of flowers, berries, fruit, shells or ribbons. Take care, however, not to overload the table with too many objects. It may be better to provide a focus in the form of a single, striking flower arrangement or a co-ordinated set of coloured glassware.

Starched white linen napkins, the bigger the better, are hard to beat. Look for them on antique stalls or flea markets – they don't have to match. Roll them into napkin rings (antique silver ones if you're fortunate enough to own them) or secure them with wide satin ribbons tied into rough knots. Ribbons edged with wire can be twisted into marvellous ornamental bows. To reflect a particular celebration or anniversary, ribbons with printed motifs can be found. Similarly, try to find napkin rings to suit the occasion. For instance, for a glamorous dinner party, pierce small squares of brightly coloured silk with pieces of wire and twist the wire around plain white napkins. Plain wooden napkin rings can be brightly painted, while inexpensive Perspex ones are available for those who favour the minimalist look.

Candles provide the best light for evening suppers or dinner parties. Use chunky church candles of different heights or tiny night lights, one for each table setting. Homemade candles in small glass jars are attractive, or, for an alfresco table setting on a metal or wooden garden table, substitute terracotta holders or containers: look out for old miniature flower pots and group them together for maximum effect. Spiky metal candlesticks of varying shapes look good grouped together, and cast atmospheric shadows on the walls.

Table-linen

Circular tablecloth

▲ *A plain wooden table tucked away in a corner of a room can all too easily fade into the background. Lit by incoming sunlight, this snugly fitted blue-and-white gingham cloth has a fresh, country-style appeal that makes the table a real focus of the room, as well as complementing the chequered china and soft furnishings.*

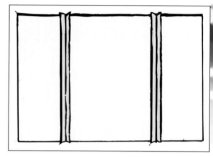

1 Join the fabric pieces, positioning a full width in the centre. Join lining pieces in same way. Press seams open.

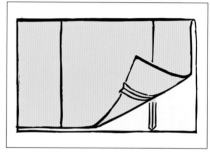

2 Fold the fabric in half, aligning the seams. The width along the fold measures the full diameter of the circle.

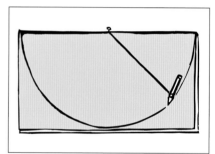

3 Mark a half-circle on folded fabric, using a pencil and a length of string. Cut lining to same shape.

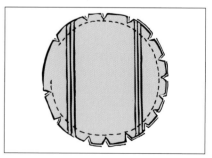

4 Pin lining to fabric and stitch, leaving an opening for turning. Trim, notch and turn right side out.

Circular tablecloths are usually decorative, and are often found covering an occasional table in the corner or at either side of a bed. Because of this they do not have to fulfil a very practical function so you can have fun with choosing different fabrics for the cloths.

Circular tablecloths

As circular tablecloths are very wide, especially those that drape right down to the floor, it is unlikely that you will find a large enough piece of fabric to cut the circle in one piece, so several widths may well need to be joined. They should never be joined down the middle as this would look unsightly on the table, but a full width of fabric should be centred and the extra widths should be added on either side of this central panel.

Making a circular tablecloth

To calculate the amount of fabric required, first measure the table's diameter and height. The basic width (diameter) of the finished cloth will equal twice the height of the table, plus the diameter of the table top. To this add 5–10cm (2–4in) to give some draping on the ground, plus an extra 3cm (1¼in) for the seam allowance around the circular edge. (Adjust if you want a shorter drop.) This gives the final width and length of fabric needed.

The lining will be the same size. Join the main fabric pieces into a square wide enough to make up the required diameter of the tablecloth, positioning a full fabric width in the centre and remembering to allow extra for seams. Press the seams open. Next, fold the fabric in half, lining up the seams. Mark the centre point along the folded edge with a pin. Tie a pencil onto the end of a length of string. Measure the length of the required radius (half the diameter) from the pencil along the string and pin the string at this point to the marked centre point. Mark out the circumference of half the circle. Cut along this half-circle through the two layers. Unfold the fabric and use it to cut a lining of the same size. (Cut an interlining if required.)

If using interlining, attach this first to the wrong side of the fabric, using large lock stitches (see page 76). With right sides together, pin the circle of fabric to the lining circle. Machine stitch 1.5cm (⅝in) from the edge, leaving an opening of about 25cm (10in) to turn the cloth right side out. Trim and notch the seam allowances and press the seam open. Turn right side out. Press under the seam allowances along the opening and slip stitch closed. Press.

Rectangular tablecloths

Straightforward rectangular tablecloths are the most versatile and are very easy to make. For an interesting variation, two covers can be made for one table – one that sits across the table widthways only and the other over the top of it lengthways only, with each cloth falling to the floor. Use contrasting colours or patterns for maximum effect – two sizes of blue check, for example.

Determining the size of a simple rectangular tablecloth couldn't be easier. All you have to do is measure the length and width of the table, and the required drop. The length of cloth required is the length of the table plus two times the drop, plus hem allowances. The width of cloth required is calculated in the same way. For neatness, hems can be hand sewn, but this can obviously be quite time-consuming and machine stitching is more practical.

Rectangular tablecloths with skirts

'Fitted' tablecloths can be made by adding a skirt or valance in much the same way that a fitted bedspread is made.

Before embarking on purchasing fabric for this type of tablecloth, you should carefully consider how the skirt will be constructed. The height of the table (that is, the drop of the skirt) is likely to be less than the standard width of fabric. Therefore if you are using plain fabric or a pattern that can be used either horizontally or vertically, you can do what is termed 'railroading' – using the width of the fabric as the drop. However, if you are using a stripe or other vertical pattern, you may have to join fabric widths in order to achieve the total length that goes around the table. Plan where your seams will be and adjust the quantity of fabric required accordingly to avoid asymmetrically placed seams.

One way to hide any necessary seams in the skirt is to position them inside the box pleats at the corners. A pleat can also be added in the centre of each long side for this purpose. An interesting detail is achieved if the pleats are cut separately and made from a contrasting fabric. If you are attempting this, be sure to position the joining seams just inside the pleat so they do not show on the pleat folds.   ▷

▲ *With each colour given equal weight, fresh citrus yellow and white marry perfectly in this kitchen. Because of the large size of the table, the yellow drape used on its own would have appeared too overpowering, upsetting the colour balance. Breaking up the mass of yellow with a smaller, white rectangular cloth restored a sense of harmony.*

▲ *A combination of tablecloths can be practical as well as decorative. This fringed green-and-white pinstriped throw is thick and hard-wearing, making it ideal for daytime use. For formal evening meals or entertaining, this protective layer can be removed to reveal the fine white linen tablecloth beneath.*

Making a rectangular tablecloth with a skirt

To calculate the amount of fabric needed, first measure the flat surface area of the table top and add a 1.5cm (⅝in) seam allowance all round. These are the dimensions for the top piece. For the skirt (which will have a kick pleat in each corner), measure each side of the table. At each corner add 20cm (8in) extra for folding into the box pleat. The total length of all the sides plus the pleat allowances and any necessary seam allowances is the required length of the skirt piece (or pieces) fabric (and lining) required. For the width of the skirt piece, measure the drop of the skirt from the edge of the table top to the floor and add 5–10cm (2–4in) to drape on the ground, plus seam allowance at both sides.

You will need enough main fabric for the top piece and the skirt and the same amount of lining fabric. Cut the table-top piece and the skirt piece (or pieces) from the main fabric and from the lining. Begin by making up the skirt. If you have several pieces of fabric for the skirt, pin and stitch them right sides together to make a large cylinder of fabric. Press the seams open. Do the same for the lining. With the right sides together, pin and stitch the lining to the fabric along one long edge. Press the seam open, then turn right side out. Press, aligning the seam along the fold. Pin the raw edges together (with wrong sides facing).

Next, pin and tack the pleats in place. The pleats must be placed precisely so that when the skirt is attached to the top of the cloth they fall exactly at each corner (and in the middle of a long side if additional pleats were made). Pin and tack the skirt to the top panel, right sides together. Machine stitch all around, making sure the pleats do not lose their position. Trim the seam allowance. Clip the seam allowance corners of the top panel piece diagonally, and notch the skirt section corners. Press the seam open and then press it towards the centre of the top.

Turn the seam allowance of the top panel lining to the wrong side and press. Pin the folded edge along the seam line where the skirt joins the top panel and hand sew it in place, using slip stitch. Turn the cloth right side out and press.

Rectangular tablecloth with skirt

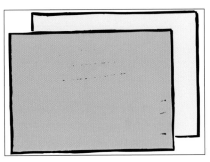

1 Cut one piece of main fabric and one piece of lining to size of table top plus seam allowance all around.

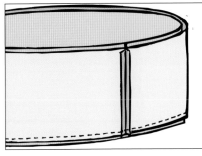

2 Cut the skirt piece (or pieces) and join into a cylinder. Make the skirt lining and join to the skirt along one edge.

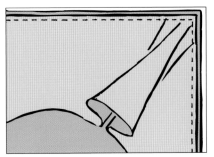

3 Turn the skirt right side out. Pin and tack the pleats at the corner positions and stitch the skirt to the top panel.

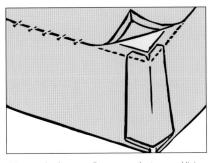

4 Press under the seam allowance on the top panel lining. Slip stitch the lining to the wrong side of the tablecloth.

Decorative square tablecloths

Arranged so that their points hang over the sides of a rectangular or square table, square tablecloths make effective drapes. They are made in the same way as simple rectangular cloths, but to determine the size you want, you will have to measure the fabric in a slightly different way. Start by deciding how far down each side of the table you wish the top cover cloth to fall. From this point, which will be the corner of the cloth, to the top of the table, doubled, is the length of each side of the cloth.

There are many simple ways to embellish a square cloth. The hem around the cover can be made with two rows of parallel stitching to add more detail. Using contrasting sewing thread will give the cloth more definition. To embellish the corners of the top cloth, if desired, attach small key tassels.

Other decorative details that can liven up plain cloths, such as fringe or braid, should be attached to the edges of the cloth by hand after the cloth is made up. A fringe should always overlap the base edge of the cloth by most of its length, allowing a few centimetres to trail on the ground. A braid applied to the edge of the cloth should line up with the finished edge. Flat braids or ribbons can also run across a square or rectangular cloth, parallel to the sides, set in about 10cm (4in) or so, and crossing at the corners to create a small square at each corner.

◄ *Napkins, place mats and flower arrangements are the finer details that can give a meal a real sense of occasion. A classic scheme of delicate white chinaware on a white linen tablecloth has been given a twist with the addition of roughly stitched, bold scarlet napkins tied with raffia coils.*

Sewing guide

Machine stitched seams

Basic flat seam

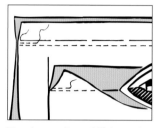

Place the two pieces of fabric together with raw edges aligned and right sides facing. Pin and tack along the edges. Remove the pins. Stitch 1.5cm (⅝in) in from the edges, working a few stitches in reverse at both ends to secure the thread. Remove the tacking and then press the seam open.

French seam

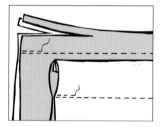

A self-neatening seam suitable for joining lightweight fabrics and for joining straight edges, French seams are ideal for items where both sides are to be visible, as no additional line of stitching will be seen. To make a French seam, place the two pieces of fabric with wrong sides together, and machine stitch a single seam 6mm (¼in) from the edge. Trim the seam allowances to 3mm (⅛in) and press the seam. Turn the fabric so that the right sides are together and press along the seam line. Next, tack a line of stitching close to the folded edge and sew a second seam 1cm (⅜in) from the folded edge. When completed, turn the fabric right sides out and finally press the seam allowance flat to one side of the finished seam.

Flat fell seam

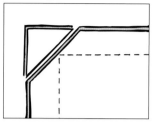

This self-neatening seam is extremely useful where strength is the essential element. With right sides together, sew 1.5cm (⅝in) from the aligned raw edges. Press the seam open. Trim one seam allowance to 6mm (¼in), fold the wide allowance over the narrow allowance and press. Fold under the edge of the wide allowance to enclose both raw edges, and top stitch close to the fold through all the layers. Press. The additional line of stitching will be visible on both sides of the fabric.

Neatening curves and corners

Clipping straight seam allowances

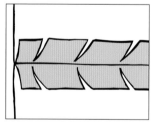

To ease tight selvages, cut into the seam allowance at approximately 5cm (2in) intervals, diagonally to the seam line and pointing downwards.

Trimming corners

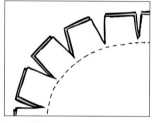

After stitching the seam, trim any corners on the diagonal, making sure you leave approximately 6mm (¼in) of the seam allowance to avoid any subsequent fraying of the fabric.

Clipping and notching curves

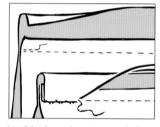

To enable curved seams to lie flat when pressed open, the seam allowances need to be clipped or notched. On inward curves, make straight clips at intervals to allow the seam allowance to open out. On outward curves, cut out tiny wedges (called 'notches') at short intervals to remove the excess bulk of the fabric.

Neatening raw edges

Pinking

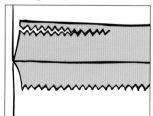

The simplest and quickest way to neaten raw edges is to use a pair of pinking shears, although it is not the most hard-wearing of methods.

Machine zigzag stitching

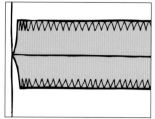

Using the zigzag setting on your machine, make a line of stitching as close to the raw edge as possible.

Self-binding (overlocking) seam

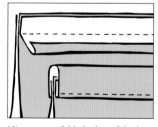

Useful where there is extra bulk – when attaching a gathered edge to a flat edge, for example. Make a seam allowance of about 3cm (1⅛in) and trim one edge to 6mm (¼in). Folding the wide edge over the narrow edge, tuck the raw edge underneath. Pin and then slip stitch along the fold.

Bias binding

Align one unfolded edge of the bias binding along the edge of the fabric and pin, tack and machine stitch along the fold of the binding. Fold the binding over the edge to the other side of the fabric, and either machine sew through all layers or slip stitch the binding in place along the stitching line. This is also a way of neatening the raw edges of fabric – the edges of tablecloths, napkins, or place mats, for example – in which case, the seam is made with wrong sides facing. If you do not want the stitches to show, slip stitch along the folded edge instead, as for a self-bound (overlocked) seam.

Oversewing by hand

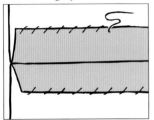

Oversewing is the best way to neaten raw edges by hand to prevent fraying. Take equal-spaced, equal-length diagonal stitches over the raw edge(s), working against the grain of the fabric.

Hems and mitring

Hems

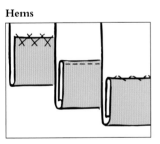

Single hems: For thick, heavy fabric, turn under the required amount of hem and press. Using herringbone stitch, sew along the edge so as to attach it to the back of the main fabric.

Double hem: A double hem secures a firm edge and is particularly suitable for sheer fabrics. Simply fold over half the hem allowance and then fold over again along the hem line. Pin, tack and finally slip stitch the hem in place.

Slip stitched hem: This hem uses less fabric than the double hem and is useful for medium-weight fabric. Turn 6mm (¼in) to the wrong side along

the raw edge and press. Fold the hem allowance to the wrong side along the hem line. Pin and tack. Finish off by slip stitching the hem into place.

Mitred corners

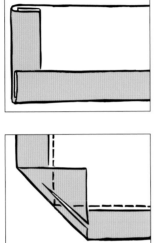

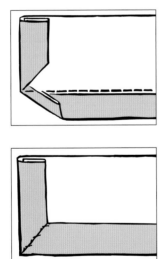

Mitred corners are used where neat corners are required. They can be made on single or double hems, and those of equal or varying widths. For single hems of equal width, turn up both side and bottom hems and press. Open out the hems, then fold in the corner of the fabric at the point where the two pressed lines cross. Check that the pressed lines on the triangle align

with those on the fabric. Turn in the hems again to form a neat join, then slip stitch the diagonal join and herringbone stitch the hems in place. For double hems of equal width, simply turn up both hems twice, unfold once, then turn in the triangle and continue as before. Both the diagonal join and the hems can be slip stitched.

When side and bottom hems are of different widths, turn in single hems and press them. Unfold the hems, but mark the limit of the turns with pins on the edge. Fold up a corner through the point where the pressed lines meet and the points marked with pins. Refold the bottom and side hems to form a neat mitre; stitch as before. For double hems of this kind, simply turn in double hems, unfold to single and mark the limit of the double turns.

Hand stitches

Running stitch

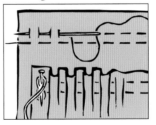

This stitch is used for simple sewing and gathering. It is worked from right to left and consists of small stitches of equal length. To gather fabric, begin on the right side of the fabric and sew two parallel lines of large running stitch. Finish each line off by winding the thread end around a pin. Pull both threads by applying even pressure to both ends of the line of sewing.

Back-stitch

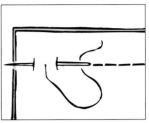

Back-stitch is useful for seams or tight corners where it is awkward to use a machine. Working from right to left, bring the needle out of the fabric and insert it a little way behind where the thread came out, then bring the needle forward the same distance in front of that point. The forward stitch will be double the length of the backward stitch. Continue in this way, making sure that you always insert the needle into the end of the last stitch so there are no gaps in the stitched line.

Ladder stitch (slip tacking)

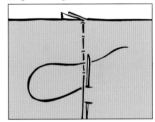

Ladder stitch, also known as slip tacking, is useful for matching patterned fabric exactly and is worked on the right side of the fabric. Press the seam allowance onto the wrong side of one piece of fabric, then with right sides upwards, place this over the unfolded seam allowance of the second piece. Pin firmly in place. With a knotted thread starting under the fold, stitch up through the fabric and across the join into the bottom piece. Next, take the needle under the fabric for a little way, then back up and across the join into the folded edge again, between the two layers of fabric. Repeat these small stitches across the join for the length of the fabric.

Slip stitch

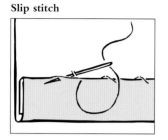

Slip stitch is used to stitch down a folded edge, such as a hem, or to join two folded edges, as in a mitred corner. In one continuous movement, working from right to left, take a tiny stitch in the main fabric, close to the previous stitch; insert the needle into the fold – about 6mm (¼in) to the left – and bring it out to the front. Continue, alternately making a tiny stitch in the main fabric and a larger stitch inside the folded edge.

Lock stitch

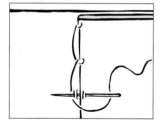

This loose stitch secures layers of fabric together – for example, holding lining and interlining in place. With wrong sides together, place the lining over the main fabric. Pin down the complete length of the fabric in the centre. Fold the fabric back against the pins.

Using matching thread, make a horizontal stitch through the folded edge and the main fabric, picking up only one or two threads of the fabric. Work at 5cm (2in) intervals down the fabric, keeping the thread very loose between the stitches. Work additional rows of lock stitch as instructed.

Herringbone stitch

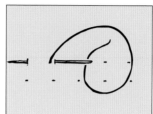

This firm stitch, worked from left to right, is used for hemming heavy-weight fabric over a single hem. Bring the thread up through the hem. Move diagonally down to the right, then take a small straight stitch just above the hem edge. Move diagonally up to the right, and take a small stitch from the hem again. Continue making crossed stitches along the length of the hem.

Blanket stitch

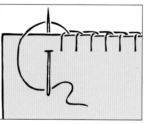

Blanket stitch can be used to neaten the edge of the fabric or as a decorative stitch when worked in a contrasting colour. Insert the needle down through the fabric at the required distance from the edge. Holding the thread under the needle point, pull the needle through at the edge, forming a loop along the edge of the fabric. Closely packed blanket stitch is used for making buttonholes.

Prick stitch

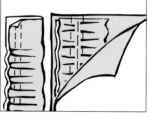

Prick stitch is used for inserting zips and for occasions where the sewing must be unobtrusive. It is sewn in the same way as backstitch, but the top stitches are smaller and should appear as pricks in the fabric. Working on the right side, take the needle back a couple of threads behind where the thread came out and then take a stitch a little way in front of that point.

Ruffles and pleats

Ruffles

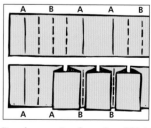

Single ruffles: Calculate the dimensions of the ruffle and add a hem and seam allowance. Cut the strip. Turn up the hem and stitch. Stitch two parallel rows of long, straight machine stitch and gather to the required length. Pin and tack to the main fabric with right sides together. Remove the pins. Machine stitch in place along the seam line and remove the tacking. Neaten the edges using machine zigzag and press upwards.

Double ruffles: To produce a full ruffle, cut double the depth of the fabric and allow twice the required top seam allowance. Fold the material in half lengthways and gather the top, as for a single ruffle.

Pleats

For each pleat allow three times the required width and remember to cut parallel to the cross grain of the fabric to ensure that the pleats hang straight.

Knife pleats

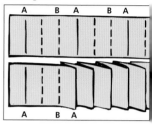

Having decided upon the required pleat width, calculate the number of pleats by measuring the edge to which the pleats will be attached and dividing by the width of the pleat. Multiply this number by three to calculate the width of fabric needed and add the seam allowances. Calculate the depth required and add seam allowances. Flat fell the seams to join the widths together and pin and stitch the hems. Mark the pleats on the fabric at right angles to the edge of the fabric. Mark the pleat line (A) and then measure twice the pleat width and mark on the placement line (B). Alternate (A) and (B) markings and measurements along the fabric. Fold the fabric on the first pleat line (A) and bring to line (B); repeat to the end of the fabric. Tack along the top of the fabric and press. Stitch in place as for ruffles.

Box pleats

Box pleats consist of two pleats folded in such a way as to turn towards each other. Begin in the same way as for knife pleats. Mark pleat line (A), measure twice the width and mark placement line (B). Then measure twice the pleat width again, to mark the next pleat line (A), then twice the width again, to the beginning of the next sequence, pleat line (A). To pleat the fabric, simply fold the two pleat lines (A) outwards to meet over the placement line. Inverted box pleats are assembled in the same way except that the pleat lines are folded inwards to meet over the placement lines.

Trimming

Piping

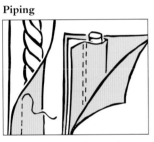

Join bias strips until they are the same length as the required length of piping cord. Place the cord on the wrong side of the strip, fold the strip over, align the edges, and first tack and then machine stitch along, close to the cord, using a zipper foot attachment. Pin the piping to the edge of the main fabric along the previous stitching line. Tack and stitch in place.

Fastenings

Buttons, hooks and studs

Buttons: Mark the position for the button and secure the thread. Slide the button over the needle and place a matchstick over the top of the

button. Work stitches through the holes of the button and over the matchstick. Remove the matchstick and pull the button up, so the slack thread is behind the button. Finish by winding the working thread around the slack to make a shank, securing the thread end inside the shank.

Hooks and eyes: Fix the eye part of the fastener every 5–10cm (2–4in) along the fabric by sewing a few stitches through each hoop. Ensure that the hooks are correctly aligned, then fix to the other side of the fabric by stitching over the neck.

Press studs: Mark the positions of the press studs by measuring every 5–10cm (2–4in) along the fabric and 6mm (¼in) from the edge. Mark the positions with pins. Sew the socket part on the seam underlap by working a few stitches through each hole. Place the ball half on the overlapping fabric and check its alignment with the socket half before securing it in place.

Fastening tapes

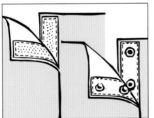

Press stud tape: This is a length of tape which has press studs fixed at set intervals along the tape. It is available in several widths.

To fix press studs, simply separate the two layers and sew the socket layer to the underneath of the fabric and the ball part to the top layer of the fabric. Stitch down the long edges of the strips, using a machine zipper foot.

Velcro: This consists of two strips of fabric, one of which has tiny hooks and the other, tiny loops. These strips stick together when pressed. Separate the two layers and stitch in place down the long edges.

Zips

Useful for cushions and chair covers, zips are available with either metal or nylon teeth and in a full range of colours, lengths and weights.

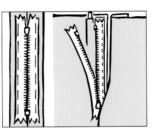

Centred zip: Stitch the seam up to the zip opening. Then tack the seam along the opening and press it open. Lay the zip downwards onto the wrong side of the fabric, exactly along the seam line, then pin and tack it in place. Turn the fabric right side up and sew the zip in place, just inside the tacking lines, using a zipper foot attachment. Fasten the threads and remove the tacking from the opening.

Zip inserted in a piped seam: Open the zip and lay one side, right side down, on the right side of the piped seam with the zip tape in the seam allowance and the zip teeth aligned with the piping. Tack and then sew in place 3mm (⅛in) from the teeth using a zipper foot attachment. Close the zip and fold back the seam allowances of both edges. Laying the plain edge on the zip, line up with the piping, pin, tack and sew in place.

Fabric ties

Flat fabric ties make a wonderful alternative to other fastenings and are useful for bed-linen and cushions. Rouleau strips – tubes made from bias strips – can be mounted as loops and used as an alternative to buttonholes.

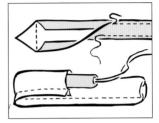

Flat ties: Cut a piece of fabric to the desired length and twice the width, adding 1cm (⅜in) all around. Folding the edges of the length to the wrong side by 1cm (⅜in), press and cut the corners at a diagonal before folding and pressing the width ends down to the wrong side. Fold the fabric in half lengthways and stitch all the sides, 3mm (⅛in) from the edge.

Rouleau ties: Fold the desired length of bias of a width of 2.5–3cm (1–1¼in) in half and sew the long edges together, 6mm (¼in) from the edge. Push a blunt-ended needle threaded with strong thread through the tube, having first secured it to one end, working along the length until it pulls through the other end. Pull the thread and the rouleau will be turned right side out. Finish by tucking the ends into the tube and then oversewing.

Stockists and suppliers

ART SUPPLIERS

Daler-Rowney
12 Percy Street
London W1A 2BP

London Graphic Centre
16–18 Shelton Street
London WC2H 9JJ

Paperchase
213 Tottenham Court Road
London W1P 9AF
(and branches)

Specialist Craft Ltd.
P.O. Box 247
Leicester LE1 9QS

Windsor and Newton
Whitefriars Avenue
Harrow
Middlesex HA3 5RH

FABRICS

Cath Kidston
8 Clarendon Cross
London W11 4AP

Designer's Guild
275–277 King's Road
London SW3 5EN

Colefax & Fowler
110 Fulham Road
London SW3 6RL

Liberty Furnishings
220 Regent Street
London W1

Osborne & Little
304 King's Road
London SW3 5UH

The Malabar Cotton Company
31–33 The South Bank
Business Centre
London SW8 5BL

Ian Mankin
109 Regent's Park Road
London NW1 8UR

Moygashel
Moygashel Mills
Moygashel
County Tyrone
Northern Ireland BT71 7QS

The Natural Fabric Company
Wessex Place
127 High Street
Hungerford
Berkshire RG17 0DL

PAINT

Brats
281 King's Road
London SW3 5EW

Cornelissen & Son Ltd.
105 Great Russell Street
London WC1B 3RY

Crown Berger Europe
P.O. Box 37
Crown House, Darwen
Lancashire BB3 0BG

Dulux
ICI Paints
Wexham Road
Slough
Berkshire SL2 5HD

Farrow & Ball Ltd.
Uddens Trading Estate
Wimborne
Dorset BH21 7NL

J.W. Bollom
13 Theobalds Road
London WC1X 8FN

Nutshell Natural Paints
Hamlyn House
Buckfastleigh
Devon TQ11 0NR

Paint Library
5 Elyston Street
London SW3 3NT

Paint Magic
116 Sheen Road
Surrey TW9 1UR

AUSTRALIA

Architectural & Design Centre
664 Botany Road
Alexandria
NSW 2015

Dulux Australia
McNaughton Road
Clayton
Victoria 3168

Home Hardware
414 Lower Dandenong Road
Braeside
Victoria 3195

McEwans
387–403 Bourke Street
Melbourne
Victoria 3000

NEW ZEALAND

Classic Upholstery
3/924 Great South Road
Penrose
Auckland

Cloth World Ltd.
4–6 Kilham Avenue
Northcote
Auckland

Cucire Designer Fabrics Ltd.
Shop 11 Harbour City Centre
Wellington

Fabric Specialists
80 Lichfield Street
Christchurch

The Fabric Warehouse
25 Hutt Road
Wellington

Material World
132 Opawa Road
Opawa
Christchurch

Uniflex Furnishings Ltd.
29 Keeling Road
Henderson
Auckland

SOUTH AFRICA

Art and Graphics Supplies
169 Oxford Road
7B Mutual Square
Rosebank
Johannesburg

Crafty Supplies
32 Main Road
Claremont
Cape

Home Warehouse
Johannesburg (Edenvale)
Dick Kemp Street
Meadowdale

Universal Paints
Randburg
24 Hendrick Verwoerd Drive
Cnr Dalmeny Road
Linden

JAPAN

Loving Design Center
Shinjuku Park Tower
3-7-1, Nishi-Shinjuku
Shinjuku-ku
Tokyo 163-10

Index

acrylic varnishes 12
appliqué 26, 28

batik 30-1
bedrooms 23
bedding 58-67
beeswax 9, 14
bias binding 44
bolster cushions 16, 42-3
borders 50-1
box cushions 36, 40-1
braid 26, 44, 49, 73
brushes
    for fabric painting 30
    for varnishing 12
built-in furniture 9
bullion fringing 44
buttons 39, 41, 45, 77
    making buttonholes 63
buying fabrics 26

calico 28, 30, 31
candles 69
canvas 28, 30, 31
chests 20, 21
children's room ideas 20, 59, 62-3, 66
cloths (tablecloths) 69-73
club armchairs 16
colour choices 9, 12
    fabrics 26, 32-3, 35, 41, 64, 69
colourwashing 7, 9, 14
combining fabrics 32-3
'copal' varnishes 12
cords, decorative 26, 44, 49
craquelure 12-13
crewelwork fabrics 28
cushions 16, 25, 32, 33, 36-43
    cushion covers 26, 44-51
customizing fabrics 26, 30-3

deck chairs 52-3
decorative finishes (furniture)
    8-23
'decorative' varnishes 12
decoupage 20-1, 66
dining chairs 54, 56-7
director's chairs 52-3
drop-in seats 54-5
dust ruffles 59, 61
duvet covers 62-3
dyeing 6, 30-1

 edgings 44
equipment for surface
        preparation (furniture) 11
ethnic fabrics 26
eyelets 45, 59, 64, 69

fabric directory 28-9
fabric ties 45, 77
fake fur 28
fastenings 45, 46, 77
floorings 16
folding stools 53
fringes 26, 44, 49, 73

glazes 13

hand stitching 75-6
hangings, bed 32, 64-5
headboards 23, 59
hooks and eyes 77

jacquard 25, 28

liming 14
linocuts on fabric 32
Lloyd Loom chairs 18
loose covers 56-7

machine stitching 74
maps decoratively on furniture 20
metal
    paint on 15
    preparation/priming of 10-11
metallic paints 9
mosaic 16, 22-3

napkins 69, 73
non-woven fabrics 28-9

oil-based varnishes 12
oil glaze 13

paint
    on fabrics 6, 30
    on metal 15
    removal of old 10-11
    on wood 14
paper on furniture 16, 18-21
patchwork 28

patinated metal effects 15
pillow cases 60-1
piping 33, 43, 44, 48-9, 77
plastic, preparation and priming
    of 11
pleated paper 19
pleating 76-7
polyurethane varnishes 12
preparation for decorative finishes
    (furniture) 10-11
press studs 45, 46, 77
priming 10-11
printed fabrics 29
printing fabrics 32-3
PVA varnish 12

ribbons 16, 26, 45, 69
rosettes 44
rouleau ties 77
round cushions 37-8, 47
ruffles 51, 76
rusted metal effects 15

 scatter cushions 36
screens, free-standing 66-7
scumble glaze 13
seams, machine-stitched 74
seating 18, 34-57
sewing guide 74-7
shellac 12
silks 6, 16, 29, 30
sofas 7, 25-6, 42
soft furnishing 24-33
sponge effects on fabric 32
square cushions 37, 39
staining wood 13
stools, folding 53
studs, upholstery 44

 tables 9, 17, 18, 19, 20, 22
    table settings 68-73
tapestry strips 45
tassels 16, 45, 49
tesserae 22-3
textured paper 19
throws 26, 57, 61
tie-on cushions 38-9
'tiles', paper-covered 20
tools see equipment
trimmings 44-5, 77
trompe l'oeil 18, 31

 valances, bed 59, 61
varnishes 9, 12
Velcro fastening 45, 46, 77
velvets 6, 29, 30
verdigris 9, 15

wallpaper paste, dyeing with 31
wallpapers for decorative effect 20
wax resists 14, 30-1
webbing, upholsterer's 55
wood
    paint/wax on 14
    preparation/priming of 10, 11
    wooden-frame screen 67
    wood stains 13
woven fabrics 25, 28-9

yarns 25

zips 45, 47, 77

Acknowledgments

The publisher would like to thank the following photographers and organizations for their kind permission to reproduce the photographs in this book.

1 Hotze Eisma; **2-3** Fritz von der Schulenburg (Mimmi O'Connell/Painter: Juliette Mole)/The Interior Archive; **4** vt wonen; **5** Mads Mogensen; **6** Ray Main; **7** *above* Henry Bourne/The World of Interiors; **7** *below* Scott Frances/Esto; **8** Trevor Richards (Kerry Skinner, Dawna Walter)/Abode; **9** Mark Luscombe-Whyte/Elizabeth Whiting & Associates; **10** Mads Mogensen; **11** Fritz von der Schulenburg/The Interior Archive; **12** Mads Mogensen; **13** Hotze Eisma; **14** Fritz von der Schulenburg (Dot Spikings)/The Interior Archive; **15** Marie-Pierre Morel (Stylist: G. Le Signe)/Marie Claire Maison; **16-17** Gilles de Chabaneix (Stylist: D. Rozensztroch)/Marie Claire Maison; **18** Trevor Richards (Kerry Skinner)/Country Homes & Interiors/Robert Harding Syndication; **19** Pierre Hussenot (Roy Comte)/Marie Claire Maison; **20** Hugh Johnson/Homes & Gardens/Robert Harding Syndication; **21** David Parmiter; **22** Geoffrey Frosh/Homes & Gardens/Robert Harding Syndication; **23** Marie-Pierre Morel (Stylist: C. Puech/G.Le Signe)/Marie Claire Maison; **24** Marie-Pierre Morel (Stylist: J. Postic)/Marie Claire Maison; **25** Dominic Blackmore/Ideal Home/Robert Harding Syndication; **26** James Merrell/Options/ Robert Harding Syndication; **27** Jan Baldwin/Options/Robert Harding Syndication; **28** *above* Nadia Mackenzie; **28** *below* Trevor Richards/Homes & Gardens/Robert Harding Syndication; **28-29** Solvi Dos Santos; **29** *above* Nadia Mackenzie; **29** *below* Designers Guild; **30** Gilles de Chabaneix (Stylist: C de Chabaneix/V. Mery)/Marie Claire Idees; **31** Christophe Dugied/Marine Archang; **32** Sandra Lane/Homes & Gardens/Robert Harding Syndication; **33** Francis Hammond (Ashley Studio); **34** Spike Powell/Elizabeth Whiting & Associates; **35** Hotze Eisma; **36** Paul Ryan/International Interiors; **37** Tim Beddow (Kelly Hoppen)/The Interior Archive; **38** Simon Brown; **39** Todd Eberle; **40** Fritz von der Schulenburg (Architect: Nico Rensch) The Interior Archive; **40-41** Kiloran Howard/Homes & Gardens/Robert Harding Syndication; **42** Jerome Darblay; **43** Christophe Dugied (Stylist: J. Postic)/Marie Claire Maison; **44** *left* Paul Ryan/International Interiors; **44** *right* Paul Warchol; **44** *below* Ariadne; **45** *left* Nadia Mackenzie; **45** *right* Ariadne; **46** Ianthe Ruthven; **48** John Hall; **49** Todd Eberle; **50** Simon Brown/Homes & Gardens/Robert Harding Syndication; **51** Hotze Eisma; **52-53** Christophe Dugied (Stylist: J.Postic)/Marie Claire Maison; **53** James Merrell/Country Homes & Interiors/Robert Harding Syndication; **54** Alexander van Berge; **55** Marie-Pierre Morel (Stylist: C.Puech)/Marie Claire Maison; **56** Laura Ashley; **58** Tom Leighton/Wedding & Home/Robert Harding Syndication; **59** Henry Wilson (Ian Dew)/The Interior Archive; **60** Tom Leighton/Wedding & Home/Robert Harding Syndication; **61** Hotze Eisma; **62** Tim Beddow (Kelly Hoppen)/The Interior Archive; **63** Hotze Eisma/v t Wonen; **64-65** Marie-Pierre Morel (Stylist: M. Bayle)/Marie Claire Maison; **66** Christophe Dugied (Stylist: J. Postic)/Marie Claire Maison; **67** Louis Gaillard (Stylist: C. Puech)/Marie Claire Maison; **68** Christophe Dugied (Stylist: J.Postic)/Marie Claire Maison; **69** Simon McBride; **70** Simon Brown; **71** Simon Upton/Options/Robert Harding Syndication; **72** Hotze Eisma; **73** Sandra Lane/Homes & Gardens/Robert Harding Syndication.